Fruits of Culture A Comedy in Four Acts, By Leo Tolstoy

Count Lev Nikolayevich Tolstoy was born on September 9th 1828 into Russian nobility but abandoned his title and through his interpretation of the ethical teachings of Jesus became a fervent Christian anarchist and pacifist. His writings on non-violence were to have a profound impact on Gandhi and Martin Luther King. His reputation for many people is based on the epic, in length and scope, of his novel 'War & Peace'. For that alone Tolstoy would be widely considered to be one of the greatest novelists of all time. But such was the breadth of his talents that he was consummate at short stories, essays and plays. Here we publish 'Fruits Of Culture' one of those classic plays.

Leo Tolstoy died acclaimed and admired throughout the world on November 20th 1910.

Table of Contents
Characters
Act 1
Act 2
Act 3
Act 4
Leo Tolstoy – A Short Biography

CHARACTERS

LEONID FYODORITCH ZVEZDINTSEF. A retired Lieutenant of the Horse Guards. Owner of more than 60,000 acres of land in various provinces. A fresh-looking, bland, agreeable gentleman of 60. Believes in Spiritualism, and likes to astonish people with his wonderful stories.

ANNA PAVLOVNA ZVEZDINTSEVA. Wife of Leonid. Stout; pretends to be young; quite taken up with the conventionalities of life; despises her husband, and blindly believes in her doctor. Very irritable.

BETSY. Their daughter. A young woman of 20, fast, tries to be mannish, wears a pince-nez, flirts and giggles. Speaks very quickly and distinctly.

VASILY LEONIDITCH ZVEZDINTSEF. Their son, aged 25; has studied law, but has no definite occupation. Member of the Cycling Club, Jockey Club, and of the Society for Promoting the Breeding of Hounds. Enjoys perfect health, and has imperturbable self-assurance. Speaks loud and abruptly. Is either perfectly serious, almost morose, or is noisily gay and laughs loud. Is nicknamed Vovo.

ALEXEY VLADIMIRITCH KROUGOSVETLOF. A professor and scientist of about 50, with quiet and pleasantly self-possessed manners, and quiet, deliberate, harmonious speech. Likes to talk. Is mildly disdainful of those who do not agree with him. Smokes much. Is lean and active.

THE DOCTOR. About 40. Healthy, fat, red-faced, loud-voiced, and rough; with a self-satisfied smile constantly on his lips.

MARYA KONSTANTINOVNA. A girl of 20, from the Conservatoire, teacher of music. Wears a fringe, and is super-fashionably dressed. Obsequious, and gets easily confused.

PETRISTCHEF. About 28; has taken his degree in philology, and is looking out for a position. Member of the same clubs as Vasily Leoniditch, and also of the Society for the Organisation of Calico Balls.[1] Is bald-headed, quick in movement and speech, and very polite.

[Note 1: Economical balls at which the ladies are bound to appear in dresses made of cotton materials.]

THE BARONESS. A pompous lady of about 50, slow in her movements, speaks with monotonous intonation.

THE PRINCESS. A society woman, a visitor.

HER DAUGHTER. An affected young society woman, a visitor.

THE COUNTESS. An ancient dame, with false hair and teeth. Moves with great difficulty.

GROSSMAN. A dark, nervous, lively man of Jewish type. Speaks very loud.

THE FAT LADY: MARYA VASILEVNA TOLBOUHINA. A very distinguished, rich, and kindly woman, acquainted with all the notable people of the last and present generations. Very stout. Speaks hurriedly, trying to be heard above every one else. Smokes.

BARON KLINGEN (nicknamed KOKO). A graduate of Petersburg University. Gentleman of the Bedchamber, Attache to an Embassy. Is perfectly correct in his deportment, and therefore enjoys peace of mind and is quietly gay.

TWO SILENT LADIES.

SERGEY IVANITCH SAHATOF. About 50, an ex-Assistant Minister of State. An elegant gentleman, of wide European culture, engaged in nothing and interested in everything. His carriage is dignified and at times even severe.

THEODORE IVANITCH. Personal attendant on Zvezdintsef, aged about 60. A man of some education and fond of information. Uses his pince-nez and pocket-handkerchief too much, unfolding the latter very slowly. Takes an interest in politics. Is kindly and sensible.

GREGORY. A footman, about 28, handsome, profligate, envious, and insolent.

JACOB. Butler, about 40, a bustling, kindly man, to whom the interests of his family in the village are all-important.

SIMON. The butler's assistant, about 20, a healthy, fresh, peasant lad, fair, beardless as yet; calm and smiling.

THE COACHMAN. A man of about 35, a dandy. Has moustaches but no beard. Rude and decided.

A DISCHARGED MAN-COOK. About 45, dishevelled, unshaved, bloated, yellow and trembling. Dressed in a ragged, light summer-overcoat and dirty trousers. Speaks hoarsely, ejecting the words abruptly.

THE SERVANTS' COOK. A talkative, dissatisfied woman of 30.

THE DOORKEEPER. A retired soldier.

TANYA (TATYANA MARKOVNA). Lady's-maid, 19, energetic, strong, merry, with quickly-changing moods. At moments, when strongly excited, she shrieks with joy.

FIRST PEASANT. About 60. Has served as village Elder. Imagines that he knows how to treat gentlefolk, and likes to hear himself talk.

SECOND PEASANT. About 45, head of a family. A man of few words. Rough and truthful. The father of Simon.

THIRD PEASANT. About 70. Wears shoes of plaited bast. Is nervous, restless, hurried, and tries to cover his confusion by much talking.

FIRST FOOTMAN (in attendance on the Countess). An old man, with old-fashioned manners, and proud of his place.

SECOND FOOTMAN. Of enormous size, strong, and rude.

A PORTER FROM A FASHIONABLE DRESSMAKER'S SHOP. A fresh-faced man in dark-blue long coat. Speaks firmly, emphatically, and clearly.

The action takes place in Moscow, in Zvezdintsef's house.

ACT I

The entrance hall of a wealthy house in Moscow. There are three doors: the front door, the door of Leonid Fyodoritch's study, and the door of Vasily Leoniditch's room. A staircase leads up to the other rooms; behind it is another door leading to the servants' quarters.

SCENE 1.

GREGORY [looks at himself in the glass and arranges his hair, &c.] I am sorry about those moustaches of mine! "Moustaches are not becoming to a footman," she says! And why? Why, so that any one might see you're a footman, else my looks might put her darling son to shame. He's a likely one! There's not much fear of his coming anywhere near me, moustaches or no moustaches! [Smiling into the glass] And what a lot of 'em swarm round me. And yet I don't care for any of them as much as for that Tanya. And she only a lady's-maid! Ah well, she's nicer than any young lady. [Smiles] She is a duck! [Listening] Ah, here she comes. [Smiles] Yes, that's her, clattering with her little heels. Oh!

[Enter Tanya, carrying a cloak and boots.]

GREGORY. My respects to you, Tatyana Markovna.

TANYA. What are you always looking in the glass for? Do you think yourself so good-looking?

GREGORY. Well, and are my looks not agreeable?

TANYA. So, so; neither agreeable nor disagreeable, but just betwixt and between! Why are all those cloaks hanging there?

GREGORY. I am just going to put them away, your ladyship! [Takes down a fur cloak and, wrapping it round her, embraces her] I say, Tanya, I'll tell you something ...

TANYA. Oh, get away, do! What do you mean by it? [Pulls herself angrily away] Leave me alone, I tell you!

GREGORY [looks cautiously around] Then give me a kiss!

TANYA. Now, really, what are you bothering for? I'll give you such a kiss! [Raises her hand to strike].

VASILY LEONIDITCH [off the scene, rings and then shouts] Gregory!

TANYA. There now, go! Vasily Leoniditch is calling you.

GREGORY. He'll wait! He's only just opened his eyes! I say, why don't you love me?

TANYA. What sort of loving have you imagined now? I don't love anybody.

GREGORY. That's a fib. You love Simon! You have found a nice one to love, a common, dirty-pawed peasant, a butler's assistant!

TANYA. Never mind; such as he is, you are jealous of him!

VASILY LEONIDITCH [off the scene] Gregory!

GREGORY. All in good time.... Jealous indeed! Of what? Why, you have only just begun to get licked into shape, and who are you tying yourself up with? Now, wouldn't it be altogether a different matter if you loved me?... I say, Tanya ...

TANYA [angrily and severely] You'll get nothing from me, I tell you!

VASILY LEONIDITCH [off the scene] Gregory!!

GREGORY. You're mighty particular, ain't you?

VASILY LEONIDITCH [off the scene, shouts persistently, monotonously, and with all his might] Gregory! Gregory! Gregory! [Tanya and Gregory laugh].

GREGORY. You should have seen the girls that have been sweet on me. [Bell rings].

TANYA. Well then, go to them, and leave me alone!

GREGORY. You are a silly, now I think of it. I'm not Simon!

TANYA. Simon means marriage, and not tomfoolery!

[Enter Porter, carrying a large cardboard box.]

PORTER. Good morning!

GREGORY. Good morning! Where are you from?

PORTER. From Bourdey's. I've brought a dress, and here's a note for the lady.

TANYA [taking the note] Sit down, and I'll take it in. [Exit].

[Vasily Leoniditch looks out of the door in shirt-sleeves and slippers.]

VASILY LEONIDITCH. Gregory!

GREGORY. Yes, sir.

VASILY LEONIDITCH. Gregory! Don't you hear me call?

GREGORY. I've only just come, sir.

VASILY LEONIDITCH. Hot water, and a cup of tea.

GREGORY. Yes, sir; Simon will bring them directly.

VASILY LEONIDITCH. And who is this? Ah, from Bourdier?

PORTER. Yes, sir.

[Exeunt Vasily Leoniditch and Gregory. Bell rings. Tanya runs in at the sound of the bell and opens the front door.]

TANYA [to Porter] Please wait a little.

PORTER. I am waiting.

[Sahatof enters at front door.]

TANYA. I beg your pardon, but the footman has just gone away. This way, sir. Allow me, please. [Takes his fur cloak].

SAHATOF [adjusting his clothes] Is Leonid Fyodoritch at home? Is he up? [Bell rings].

TANYA. Oh yes, sir. He's been up a long time.

[Doctor enters and looks round for the footman. Sees Sahatof and addresses him in an offhand manner.]

DOCTOR. Ah, my respects to you!

SAHATOF [looks fixedly at him] The Doctor, I believe?

DOCTOR. And I thought you were abroad! Dropped in to see Leonid Fyodoritch?

SAHATOF. Yes. And you? Is any one ill?

DOCTOR [laughing] Not exactly ill, but, you know ... It's awful with these ladies! Sits up at cards till three every morning, and pulls her waist into the shape of a wine-glass. And the lady is flabby and fat, and carries the weight of a good many years on her back.

SAHATOF. Is this the way you state your diagnosis to Anna Pavlovna? I should hardly think it quite pleases her!

DOCTOR [laughing] Well, it's the truth. They do all these tricks, and then come derangements of the digestive organs, pressure on the liver, nerves, and all sorts of things, and one has to come and patch them up. It's just awful! [Laughs] And you? You are also a spiritualist it seems?

SAHATOF. I? No, I am not also a spiritualist.... Good morning! [Is about to go, but is stopped by the Doctor].

DOCTOR. No! But I can't myself, you know, positively deny the possibility of it, when a man like Krougosvetlof is connected with it all. How can one? Is he not a professor, a European celebrity? There must be something in it. I should like to see for myself, but I never have the time. I have other things to do.

SAHATOF. Yes, yes! Good morning. [Exit, bowing slightly].

DOCTOR [to Tanya] Is Anna Pavlovna up?

TANYA. She's in her bedroom, but please come up.

[Doctor goes upstairs.]

[Theodore Ivanitch enters with a newspaper in his hand.]

THEODORE IVANITCH [to Porter] What is it you want?

PORTER. I'm from Bourdey's. I brought a dress and a note, and was told to wait.

THEODORE IVANITCH. Ah, from Bourdey's! [To Tanya] Who came in just now?

TANYA. It was Sergey Ivanitch Sahatof and the Doctor. They stood talking here a bit. It was all about spiritalism.

THEODORE IVANITCH [correcting her] Spiritualism.

TANYA. Yes, that's just what I said, spiritalism. Have you heard how well it went off last time, Theodore Ivanitch? [Laughs] There was knocks, and things flew about!

THEODORE IVANITCH. And how do you know?

TANYA. Miss Elizabeth told me.

[Jacob runs in with a tumbler of tea on a tray.]

JACOB [to the Porter] Good morning!

PORTER [disconsolately] Good morning!

[Jacob knocks at Vasily Leoniditch's door.]

[Gregory enters.]

GREGORY. Give it here.

JACOB. You didn't bring back all yesterday's tumblers, nor the tray Vasily Leoniditch had. And it's me that have to answer for them!

GREGORY. The tray is full of cigars.

JACOB. Well, put them somewhere else. It's me who's answerable for it.

GREGORY. I'll bring it back! I'll bring it back!

JACOB. Yes, so you say, but it is not where it ought to be. The other day, just as the tea had to be served, it was not to be found.

GREGORY. I'll bring it back, I tell you. What a fuss!

JACOB. It's easy for you to talk. Here am I serving tea for the third time, and now there's the lunch to get ready. One does nothing but rush about the livelong day. Is there any one in the house who has more to do than me? Yet they are never satisfied with me.

GREGORY. Dear me? Who could wish for any one more satisfactory? You're such a fine fellow!

TANYA. Nobody is good enough for you! You alone ...

GREGORY [to Tanya] No one asked your opinion! [Exit].

JACOB. Ah well, I don't mind. Tatyana Markovna, did the mistress say anything about yesterday?

TANYA. About the lamp, you mean?

JACOB. And how it managed to drop out of my hands, the Lord only knows! Just as I began rubbing it, and was going to take hold of it in another place, out it slips and goes all to pieces. It's just my luck! It's easy for that Gregory Mihaylitch to talk, a single man like him! But when one has a family, one has to consider things: they have to be fed. I don't mind work.... So she didn't say anything? The Lord be thanked!... Oh, Theodore Ivanitch, have you one spoon or two?

THEODORE IVANITCH. One. Only one! [Reads newspaper].

[Exit Jacob.]

[Bell rings. Enter Gregory (carrying a tray) and the Doorkeeper.]

DOORKEEPER [to Gregory] Tell the master some peasants have come from the village.

GREGORY [pointing to Theodore Ivanitch] Tell the major-domo here, it's his business. I have no time. [Exit].

TANYA. Where are these peasants from?

DOORKEEPER. From Koursk, I think.

TANYA [shrieks with delight] It's them.... It's Simon's father come about the land! I'll go and meet them! [Runs off].

DOORKEEPER. Well, then, what shall I say to them? Shall they come in here? They say they've come about the land, the master knows, they say.

THEODORE IVANITCH. Yes, they want to purchase some land. All right! But he has a visitor now, so you had better tell them to wait.

DOORKEEPER. Where shall they wait?

THEODORE IVANITCH. Let them wait outside. I'll send for them when the time comes. [Exit Doorkeeper]

[Enter Tanya, followed by three Peasants.]

TANYA. To the right. In here! In here!

THEODORE IVANITCH. I did not want them brought in here!

GREGORY. Forward minx!

TANYA. Oh, Theodore Ivanitch, it won't matter, they'll stand in this corner.

THEODORE IVANITCH. They'll dirty the floor.

TANYA. They've scraped their shoes, and I'll wipe the floor up afterwards. [To Peasants] Here, stand just here.

[Peasants come forward carrying presents tied in cotton handkerchiefs: cake, eggs, and embroidered towels. They look around for an icon before which to cross themselves; not finding one, they cross themselves looking at the staircase.]

GREGORY [to Theodore Ivanitch]. There now, Theodore Ivanitch, they say Pironnet's boots are an elegant shape. But those there are ever so much better. [Pointing to the third Peasant's bast shoes].

THEODORE IVANITCH. Why will you always be ridiculing people? [Exit Gregory].

THEODORE IVANITCH [rises and goes up to the Peasants] So you are from Koursk? And have come to arrange about buying some land?

FIRST PEASANT. Just so. We might say, it is for the completion of the purchase of the land we have come. How could we announce ourselves to the master?

THEODORE IVANITCH. Yes, yes, I know. You wait a bit and I'll go and inform him. [Exit].

[The Peasants look around; they are embarrassed where to put their presents.]

FIRST PEASANT. There now, couldn't we have what d'you call it? Something to present these here things on? To do it in a genteel way, like, a little dish or something.

TANYA. All right, directly; put them down here for the present. [Puts bundles on settle].

FIRST PEASANT. There now, that respectable gentleman that was here just now, what might be his station?

TANYA. He's the master's valet.

FIRST PEASANT. I see. So he's also in service. And you, now, are you a servant too?

TANYA. I am lady's-maid. Do you know, I also come from Demen! I know you, and you, but I don't know him. [Pointing to third Peasant].

THIRD PEASANT. Them two you know, but me you don't know?

TANYA. You are Efim Antonitch.

FIRST PEASANT. That's just it!

TANYA. And you are Simon's father, Zachary Trifanitch.

SECOND PEASANT. Right!

THIRD PEASANT. And let me tell you, I'm Mitry Vlasitch Tchilikin. Now do you know?

TANYA. Now I shall know you too!

SECOND PEASANT. And who may you be?

TANYA. I am Aksinya's, the soldier's wife's, orphan.

FIRST AND THIRD PEASANTS [with surprise] Never!

SECOND PEASANT. The proverb says true:

"Buy a penny pig, put it in the rye,
And you'll have a wonderful fat porker by-and-by."

FIRST PEASANT. That's just it! She's got the resemblance of a duchess!

THIRD PEASANT. That be so truly. Oh Lord!

VASILY LEONIDITCH. [off the scene, rings, and then shouts] Gregory! Gregory!

FIRST PEASANT. Now who's that, for example, disturbing himself in such a way, if I may say so?

TANYA. That's the young master.

THIRD PEASANT. Oh Lord! Didn't I say we'd better wait outside until the time comes? [Silence].

SECOND PEASANT. Is it you, Simon wants to marry?

TANYA. Why, has he been writing? [Hides her face in her apron].

SECOND PEASANT. It's evident he's written! But it's a bad business he's imagined here. I see the lad's got spoilt!

TANYA [quickly] No, he's not at all spoilt! Shall I send him to you?

SECOND PEASANT. Why send him? All in good time. Where's the hurry?

VASILY LEONIDITCH [desperately, behind scene] Gregory! Where the devil are you?... [Enters from his room in shirt-sleeves, adjusting his pince-nez].

VASILY LEONIDITCH. Is every one dead?

TANYA. He's not here, sir.... I'll send him to you at once. [Moves towards the back door].

VASILY LEONIDITCH. I could hear you talking, you know. How have these scarecrows sprung up here? Eh? What?

TANYA. They're peasants from the Koursk village, sir. [Peasants bow].

VASILY LEONIDITCH. And who is this? Oh yes, from Bourdier.

[Vasily Leoniditch pays no attention to the Peasants' bow. Tanya meets Gregory at the doorway and remains on the scene.]

VASILY LEONIDITCH [to Gregory] I told you the other boots... I can't wear these!

GREGORY. Well, the others are also there.

VASILY LEONIDITCH. But where is there?

GREGORY. Just in the same place!

VASILY LEONIDITCH. They're not!

GREGORY. Well, come and see. [Exeunt Gregory and Vasily Leoniditch].

THIRD PEASANT. Say now, might we not in the meantime just go and wait, say, in some lodging-house or somewhere?

TANYA. No, no, wait a little. I'll go and bring you some plates to put the presents on. [Exit].

[Enter Sahatof and Leonid Fyodoritch, followed by Theodore Ivanitch.]

[The Peasants take up the presents, and pose themselves.]

LEONID FYODORITCH [to Peasants] Presently, presently! Wait a bit! [Points to Porter] Who is this?

PORTER. From Bourdey's.

LEONID FYODORITCH. Ah, from Bourdier.

SAHATOF [smiling] Well, I don't deny it: still you understand that, never having seen it, we, the uninitiated, have some difficulty in believing.

LEONID FYODORITCH. You say you find it difficult to believe! We do not ask for faith; all we demand of you is to investigate! How can I help believing in this ring? Yet this ring came from there!

SAHATOF. From there? What do you mean? From where?

LEONID FYODORITCH. From the other world. Yes!

SAHATOF [smiling] That's very interesting, very interesting!

LEONID FYODORITCH. Well, supposing we admit that I'm a man carried away by an idea, as you think, and that I am deluding myself. Well, but what of Alexey Vladimiritch Krougosvetlof, he is not just an ordinary man, but a distinguished professor, and yet he admits it to be a fact. And not he alone. What of Crookes? What of Wallace?

SAHATOF. But I don't deny anything. I only say it is very interesting. It would be interesting to know how Krougosvetlof explains it!

LEONID FYODORITCH. He has a theory of his own. Could you come to-night? he is sure to be here. First we shall have Grossman, you know, the famous thought-reader?

SAHATOF. Yes, I have heard of him but have never happened to meet him.

LEONID FYODORITCH. Then you must come! We shall first have Grossman, then Kaptchitch, and our mediumistic seance.... [To Theodore Ivanitch] Has the man returned from Kaptchitch?

THEODORE IVANITCH. Not yet, sir.

SAHATOF. Then how am I to know?

LEONID FYODORITCH. Never mind, come in any case! If Kaptchitch can't come we shall find our own medium. Marya Ignatievna is a medium, not such a good one as Kaptchitch, but still ...

[Tanya enters with plates for the presents, and stands listening.]

SAHATOF [smiling] Oh yes, yes. But here is one puzzling point: how is it that the mediums are always of the, so-called, educated class, such as Kaptchitch and Marya Ignatievna? If there were such a special force, would it not be met with also among the common people, the peasants?

LEONID FYODORITCH. Oh yes, and it is! That is very common. Even here in our own house we have a peasant whom we discovered to be a medium. A few days ago we called him in, a sofa had to be moved, during a seance, and we forgot all about him. In all probability he fell asleep. And, fancy, after our seance was over and Kaptchitch had come to again, we suddenly noticed mediumistic phenomena in another part of the room, near the peasant: the table gave a jerk and moved!

TANYA [aside] That was when I was getting out from under it!

LEONID FYODORITCH. It is quite evident he also is a medium. Especially as he is very like Home in appearance. You remember Home, a fair-haired naïve sort of fellow?

SAHATOF [shrugging his shoulders] Dear me, this is very interesting, you know. I think you should try him.

LEONID FYODORITCH. So we will! And he is not alone; there are thousands of mediums, only we do not know them. Why, only a short time ago a bedridden old woman moved a brick wall!

SAHATOF. Moved a brick ... a brick wall?

LEONID FYODORITCH. Yes, yes. She was lying in bed, and did not even know she was a medium. She just leant her arm against the wall, and the wall moved!

SAHATOF. And did not cave in?

LEONID FYODORITCH. And did not cave in.

SAHATOF. Very strange! Well then, I'll come this evening.

LEONID FYODORITCH. Pray do. We shall have a seance in any case. [Sahatof puts on his outdoor things, Leonid Fyodoritch sees him to the door].

PORTER [to Tanya] Do tell your mistress! Am I to spend the night here?

TANYA. Wait a little; she's going to drive out with the young lady, so she'll soon be coming downstairs. [Exit].

LEONID FYODORITCH [comes up to the Peasants, who bow and offer him their presents] That's not necessary!

FIRST PEASANT [smiling] Oh, but this-here is our first duty, it is! It's also the Commune's orders that we should do it!

SECOND PEASANT. That's always been the proper way.

THIRD PEASANT. Say no more about it! 'Cause as we are much satisfied.... As our parents, let's say, served, let's say, your parents, so we would like the same with all our hearts ... and not just anyhow! [Bows].

LEONID FYODORITCH. But what is it about? What do you want?

FIRST PEASANT. It's to your honour we've come ...

[Enter Petristchef briskly, in fur-lined overcoat.]

PETRISTCHEF. Is Vasily Leoniditch awake yet? [Seeing Leonid Fyodoritch, bows, moving only his head].

LEONID FYODORITCH. You have come to see my son?

PETRISTCHEF. I? Yes, just to see Vovo for a moment.

LEONID FYODORITCH. Step in, step in.

[Petristchef takes off his overcoat and walks in briskly. Exit.]

LEONID FYODORITCH [to Peasants] Well, what is it you want?

SECOND PEASANT. Please accept our presents!

FIRST PEASANT [smiling] That's to say, the peasants' offerings.

THIRD PEASANT. Say no more about it; what's the good? We wish you the same as if you were our own father! Say no more about it!

LEONID FYODORITCH. All right. Here, Theodore, take these.

THEODORE IVANITCH [to Peasants] Give them here. [Takes the presents].

LEONID FYODORITCH. Well, what is the business?

FIRST PEASANT. We've come to your honour ...

LEONID FYODORITCH. I see you have; but what do you want?

FIRST PEASANT. It's about making a move towards completing the sale of the land. It comes to this ...

LEONID FYODORITCH. Do you mean to buy the land?

FIRST PEASANT. That's just it. It comes to this ... I mean the buying of the property of the land. The Commune has given us, let's say, the power of atturning, to enter, let's say, as is lawful, through the Government bank, with a stamp for the lawful amount.

LEONID FYODORITCH. You mean that you want to buy the land through the land-bank.

FIRST PEASANT. That's just it. Just as you offered it to us last year. It comes to this, then, the whole sum in full for the buying of the property of the land is 32,864 roubles.

LEONID FYODORITCH. That's all right, but how about paying up?

FIRST PEASANT. As to the payment, the Commune offers just as it was said last year, to pay in 'stalments, and your receipt of the ready money by lawful regulations, 4000 roubles in full.[2]

[Note 2: The present value of the rouble is rather over two shillings and one penny.]

SECOND PEASANT. Take 4000 now, and wait for the rest of the money.

THIRD PEASANT [unwrapping a parcel of money] And about this be quite easy. We should pawn our own selves rather than do such a thing just anyhow say, but in this way, let's say, as it ought to be done.

LEONID FYODORITCH. But did I not write and tell you that I should not agree to it unless you brought the whole sum?

FIRST PEASANT. That's just it. It would be more agreeable, but it is not in our possibilities, I mean.

LEONID FYODORITCH. Well then, the thing can't be done!

FIRST PEASANT. The Commune, for example, relied its hopes on that, that you made the offer last year to sell it in easy 'stalments ...

LEONID FYODORITCH. That was last year. I would have agreed to it then, but now I can't.

SECOND PEASANT. But how's that? We've been depending on your promise, we've got the papers ready and have collected the money!

THIRD PEASANT. Be merciful, master! We're short of land; we'll say nothing about cattle, but even a hen, let's say, we've no room to keep. [Bows] Don't wrong us, master! [Bows].

LEONID FYODORITCH. Of course it's quite true, that I agreed last year to let you have the land for payment by instalments, but now circumstances are such that it would be inconvenient.

SECOND PEASANT. Without this land we cannot live!

FIRST PEASANT. That's just it. Without land our lives must grow weaker and come to a decline.

THIRD PEASANT [bowing] Master, we have so little land, let's not talk about the cattle, but even a chicken, let's say, we've no room for. Master, be merciful, accept the money, master!

LEONID FYODORITCH [examining the document] I quite understand, and should like to help you. Wait a little; I will give you an answer in half-an-hour.... Theodore, say I am engaged and am not to be disturbed.

THEODORE IVANITCH. Yes, sir. [Exit Leonid Fyodoritch].

[The Peasants look dejected.]

SECOND PEASANT. Here's a go! "Give me the whole sum," he says. And where are we to get it from?

FIRST PEASANT. If he had not given us hopes, for example. As it is we felt quite insured it would be as was said last year.

THIRD PEASANT. Oh Lord! and I had begun unwrapping the money. [Begins wrapping up the bundle of bank-notes again] What are we to do now?

THEODORE IVANITCH. What is your business, then?

FIRST PEASANT. Our business, respected sir, depends in this. Last year he made us the offer of our buying the land in 'stalments. The Commune entered upon these terms and gave us the powers of atturning, and now d'you see he makes the offering that we should pay the whole in full! And as it turns out, the business is no ways convenient for us.

THEODORE IVANITCH. What is the whole sum?

FIRST PEASANT. The whole sum in readiness is 4000 roubles, you see.

THEODORE IVANITCH. Well, what of that? Make an effort and collect more.

FIRST PEASANT. Such as it is, it was collected with much effort. We have, so to say, in this sense, not got ammunition enough.

SECOND PEASANT. You can't get blood out of a stone.

THIRD PEASANT. We'd be glad with all our hearts, but we have swept even this together, as you might say, with a broom.

[Vasily Leoniditch and Petristchef appear in the doorway both smoking cigarettes.]

VASILY LEONIDITCH. I have told you already I'll do my best, so of course I will do all that is possible! Eh, what?

PETRISTCHEF. You must just understand that if you do not get it, the devil only knows what a mess we shall be in!

VASILY LEONIDITCH. But I've already said I'll do my best, and so I will. Eh, what?

PETRISTCHEF. Nothing. I only say, get some at any cost. I will wait.

[Exit into Vasily Leoniditch's room, closing door.]

VASILY LEONIDITCH [waving his arm] It's a deuce of a go! [The Peasants bow].

VASILY LEONIDITCH [looking at Porter, to Theodore Ivanitch] Why don't you attend to this fellow from Bourdier? He hasn't come to take lodgings with us, has he? Just look, he is asleep! Eh, what?

THEODORE IVANITCH. The note he brought has been sent in, and he has been told to wait until Anna Pavlovna comes down.

VASILY LEONIDITCH [looks at Peasants and notices the money] And what is this? Money? For whom? Is it for us? [To Theodore Ivanitch] Who are they?

THEODORE IVANITCH. They are peasants from Koursk. They are buying land.

VASILY LEONIDITCH. Has it been sold them?

THEODORE IVANITCH. No, they have not yet come to any agreement. They are too stingy.

VASILY LEONIDITCH. Eh? Well, we must try and persuade them. [To the Peasants] Here, I say, are you buying land? Eh?

FIRST PEASANT. That's just it. We have made an offering as how we should like to acquire the possession of the land.

VASILY LEONIDITCH. Then you should not be so stingy, you know. Just let me tell you how necessary land is to peasants! Eh, what? It's very necessary, isn't it?

FIRST PEASANT. That's just it. The land appears as the very first and foremost necessity to a peasant. That's just it.

VASILY LEONIDITCH. Then why be so stingy? Just you think what land is! Why, one can sow wheat on it in rows! I tell you, you could get eighty bushels of wheat, at a rouble and a half a bushel, that would be 120 roubles. Eh, what? Or else mint! I tell you, you could collar 400 roubles off an acre by sowing mint!

FIRST PEASANT. That's just it. All sorts of producks one could put into action if one had the right understanding.

VASILY LEONIDITCH. Mint! Decidedly mint! I have learnt about it, you know. It's all printed in books. I can show them you. Eh, what?

FIRST PEASANT. That's just it, all concerns are clearer to you through your books. That's learnedness, of course.

VASILY LEONIDITCH. Then pay up and don't be stingy. [To Theodore Ivanitch] Where's papa?

THEODORE IVANITCH. He gave orders not to be disturbed just now.

VASILY LEONIDITCH. Oh, I suppose he's consulting a spirit whether to sell the land or not? Eh, what?

THEODORE IVANITCH. I can't say. All I know is that he went away undecided about it.

VASILY LEONIDITCH. What d'you think, Theodore Ivanitch, is he flush of cash? Eh, what?

THEODORE IVANITCH. I don't know. I hardly think so. But what does it matter to you? You drew a good sum not more than a week ago.

VASILY LEONIDITCH. But didn't I pay for those dogs? And now, you know, there's our new Society, and Petristchef has been chosen, and I had borrowed money from Petristchef and must pay the subscription both for him and for myself. Eh, what?

THEODORE IVANITCH. And what is this new Society? A Cycling Club?

VASILY LEONIDITCH. No. Just let me tell you. It is quite a new Society. It is a very serious Society, you know. And who do you think is President? Eh, what?

THEODORE IVANITCH. What's the object of this new Society?

VASILY LEONIDITCH. It is a "Society to Promote the Breeding of Pure-bred Russian Hounds." Eh, what? And I'll tell you, they're having the first meeting and a lunch, to-day. And I've no money. I'll go to him and have a try! [Exit through study door].

FIRST PEASANT [to Theodore Ivanitch] And who might he be, respected sir?

THEODORE IVANITCH [smiles] The young master.

THIRD PEASANT. The heir, so to say. Oh Lord! [puts away the money] I'd better hide it meanwhile.

FIRST PEASANT. And we were told he was in military service, in the cav'rely, for example.

THEODORE IVANITCH. No, as an only son he is exempt from military service.

THIRD PEASANT. Left for to keep his parents, so to say! That's right!

SECOND PEASANT [shaking his head] He's the right sort. He'll feed them finely!

THIRD PEASANT. Oh Lord!

[Enter Vasily Leoniditch followed by Leonid Fyodoritch.]

VASILY LEONIDITCH. That's always the way. It's really surprising! First I'm asked why I have no occupation, and now when I have found a field and am occupied, when a Society with serious and noble aims has been founded, I can't even have 300 roubles to go on with!...

LEONID FYODORITCH. I tell you I can't do it, and I can't! I haven't got it.

VASILY LEONIDITCH. Why, you have just sold some land.

LEONID FYODORITCH. In the first place I have not sold it! And above all, do leave me in peace! Weren't you told I was engaged? [Exit, slamming door].

THEODORE IVANITCH. I told you this was not the right moment.

VASILY LEONIDITCH. Well, I say! Here's a position to be in! I'll go and see mamma, that's my only hope. He's going crazy over his spiritualism and forgets everything else. [Goes upstairs].

[Theodore Ivanitch takes newspaper and is just going to sit down, when Betsy and Marya Konstantinovna, followed by Gregory, come down the stairs.]

BETSY. Is the carriage ready?

GREGORY. Just coming to the door.

BETSY [to Marya Konstantinovna] Come along, come along, I know it is he.

MARYA KONSTANTINOVNA. Which he?

BETSY. You know very well whom I mean, Petristchef, of course.

MARYA KONSTANTINOVNA. But where is he?

BETSY. Sitting in Vovo's room. You'll see!

MARYA KONSTANTINOVNA. And suppose it is not he? [The Peasants and Porter bow].

BETSY [to Porter] You brought a dress from Bourdier's?

PORTER. Yes, Miss. May I go?

BETSY. Well, I don't know. Ask my mother.

PORTER. I don't know whose it is, Miss; I was ordered to bring it here and receive the money.

BETSY. Well then, wait.

MARYA KONSTANTINOVNA. Is it still that costume for the charade?

BETSY. Yes, a charming costume. But mamma won't take it or pay for it.

MARYA KONSTANTINOVNA. But why not?

BETSY. You'd better ask mamma. She doesn't grudge Vovo 500 roubles for his dogs, but 100 is too much for a dress. I can't act dressed like a scarecrow. [Pointing to Peasants] And who are these?

GREGORY. Peasants who have come to buy some land or other.

BETSY. And I thought they were the beaters. Are you not beaters?

FIRST PEASANT. No, no, lady. We have come to see Leonid Fyodoritch about the signing into our possession of the title-deeds to some land.

BETSY. Then how is it? Vovo was expecting some beaters who were to come to-day. Are you sure you are not the beaters? [The Peasants are silent] How stupid they are! [Goes to Vasily Leoniditch's door] Vovo? [Laughs].

MARYA KONSTANTINOVNA. But we met him just now upstairs!

BETSY. Why need you remember that? Vovo, are you there?

[Petristchef enters.]

PETRISTCHEF. Vovo is not here, but I am prepared to fulfil on his behalf anything that may be required. How do you do? How do you do, Marya Konstantinovna? [Shakes hands long and violently with Betsy, and then with Marya Konstantinovna].

SECOND PEASANT. See, it's as if he were pumping water!

BETSY. You can't replace him, still you're better than nobody. [Laughs] What are these affairs of yours with Vovo?

PETRISTCHEF. What affairs? Our affairs are fie-nancial, that is, our business is fie! It's also nancial, and besides it is financial.

BETSY. What does nancial mean?

PETRISTCHEF. What a question! It means nothing, that's just the point.

BETSY. No, no, you have missed fire. [Laughs].

PETRISTCHEF. One can't always hit the mark, you know. It's something like a lottery. Blanks and blanks again, and at last you win! [Theodore Ivanitch goes into the study].

BETSY. Well, this was blank then; but tell me, were you at the Mergasofs' last night?

PETRISTCHEF. Not exactly at the Mere Gasof's, but rather at the Pere Gasof's, or better still, at the Fils Gasof's.

BETSY. You can't do without puns. It's an illness. And were the Gypsies there?[3] [Laughs].

[Note 3: The Gypsy choirs are very popular in Moscow.]

PETRISTCHEF [sings] "On their aprons silken threads, little birds with golden heads!" ...

BETSY. Happy mortals! And we were yawning at Fofo's.

PETRISTCHEF [continues to sing] "And she promised and she swore, She would ope' her ... her ... her ..." how does it go on, Marya Konstantinovna?

MARYA KONSTANTINOVNA. "Closet door."

PETRISTCHEF. How? What? How, Marya Konstantinovna?

BETSY. Cessez, vous devenez impossible![4]

[Note: 4 BETSY. Cease! You are becoming quite unbearable!]

PETRISTCHEF. J'ai cesse, j'ai bebe, j'ai dede....[5]

[Note 5: PETRISTCHEF. I have C said (ceased), B said, and D said.]

BETSY. I see the only way to rid ourselves of your wit is to make you sing! Let us go into Vovo's room, his guitar is there. Come, Marya Konstantinovna, come! [Exeunt Betsy, Marya Konstantinovna, and Petristchef].

FIRST PEASANT. Who be they?

GREGORY. One is our young lady, the other is a girl who teaches her music.

FIRST PEASANT. Administrates learning, so to say. And ain't she smart? A reg'lar picture!

SECOND PEASANT. Why don't they marry her? She is old enough, I should say.

GREGORY. Do you think it's the same as among you peasants, marry at fifteen?

FIRST PEASANT. And that man, for example, is he also in the musitional line?

GREGORY [mimicking him] "Musitional" indeed! You don't understand anything!

FIRST PEASANT. That's just so. And stupidity, one might say, is our ignorance.

THIRD PEASANT. Oh Lord! [Gipsy songs and guitar accompaniment are heard from Vasily Leoniditch's room].

[Enter Simon, followed by Tanya, who watches the meeting between father and son.]

GREGORY [to Simon] What do you want?

SIMON. I have been to Mr. Kaptchitch.

GREGORY. Well, and what's the answer?

SIMON. He sent word he couldn't possibly come to-night.

GREGORY. All right, I'll let them know. [Exit].

SIMON [to his father] How d'you do, father! My respects to Daddy Efim and Daddy Mitry! How are all at home?

SECOND PEASANT. Very well, Simon.

FIRST PEASANT. How d'you do, lad?

THIRD PEASANT. How d'you do, sonny?

SIMON [smiles] Well, come along, father, and have some tea.

SECOND PEASANT. Wait till we've finished our business. Don't you see we are not ready yet?

SIMON. Well, I'll wait for you by the porch. [Wishes to go away].

TANYA [running after him] I say, why didn't you tell him anything?

SIMON. How could I before all those people? Give me time, I'll tell him over our tea. [Exit].

[Theodore Ivanitch enters and sits down by the window.]

FIRST PEASANT. Respected sir, how's our business proceeding?

THEODORE IVANITCH. Wait a bit, he'll be out presently, he's just finishing.

TANYA [to Theodore Ivanitch] And how do you know, Theodore Ivanitch, he is finishing?

THEODORE IVANITCH. I know that when he has finished questioning, he reads the question and answer aloud.

TANYA. Can one really talk with spirits by means of a saucer?

THEODORE IVANITCH. It seems so.

TANYA. But supposing they tell him to sign, will he sign?

THEODORE IVANITCH. Of course he will.

TANYA. But they do not speak with words?

THEODORE IVANITCH. Oh, yes. By means of the alphabet. He notices at which letter the saucer stops.

TANYA. Yes, but at a si-ance?...

[Enter Leonid Fyodoritch.]

LEONID FYODORITCH. Well, friends, I can't do it! I should be very glad to, but it is quite impossible. If it were for ready money it would be a different matter.

FIRST PEASANT. That's just so. What more could any one desire? But the people are so inpennycuous, it is quite impossible!

LEONID FYODORITCH. Well, I can't do it, I really can't. Here is your document; I can't sign it.

THIRD PEASANT. Show some pity, master; be merciful!

SECOND PEASANT. How can you act so? It is doing us a wrong.

LEONID FYODORITCH. Nothing wrong about it, friends. I offered it you in summer, but then you did not agree; and now I can't agree to it.

THIRD PEASANT. Master, be merciful! How are we to get along? We have so little land. We'll say nothing about the cattle; a hen, let's say, there's no room to let a hen run about.

[Leonid Fyodoritch goes up to the door and stops. Enter, descending the staircase, Anna Pavlovna and doctor, followed by Vasily Leoniditch, who is in a merry and playful mood and is putting some bank-notes into his purse.]

ANNA PAVLOVNA [tightly laced, and wearing a bonnet] Then I am to take it?

DOCTOR. If the symptoms recur you must certainly take it, but above all, you must behave better. How can you expect thick syrup to pass through a thin little hair tube, especially when we squeeze the tube? It's impossible; and so it is with the biliary duct. It's simple enough.

ANNA PAVLOVNA. All right, all right!

DOCTOR. Yes, "All right, all right," and you go on in the same old way. It won't do, madam, it won't do. Well, good-bye!

ANNA PAVLOVNA. No, not good-bye, only au revoir! For I still expect you to-night. I shall not be able to make up my mind without you.

DOCTOR. All right, if I have time I'll pop in. [Exit].

ANNA PAVLOVNA [noticing the Peasants] What's this? What? What people are these? [Peasants bow].

THEODORE IVANITCH. These are peasants from Koursk, come to see Leonid Fyodoritch about the sale of some land.

ANNA PAVLOVNA. I see they are peasants, but who let them in?

THEODORE IVANITCH. Leonid Fyodoritch gave the order. He has just been speaking to them about the sale of the land.

ANNA PAVLOVNA. What sale? There is no need to sell any. But above all, how can one let in people from the street into the house? One can't let people in from the street! One can't let people into the house who have spent the night heaven knows where!... [Getting more and more excited] I daresay every fold of their clothes is full of microbes, of scarlet-fever microbes, of smallpox microbes, of diphtheria microbes! Why, they are from Koursk Government, where there is an epidemic of diphtheria ... Doctor! Doctor! Call the doctor back!

[Leonid Fyodoritch goes into his room and shuts the door. Gregory goes to recall the Doctor.]

VASILY LEONIDITCH [smokes at the Peasants] Never mind, mamma; if you like I'll fumigate them so that all the microbes will go to pot! Eh, what?

[Anna Pavlovna remains severely silent, awaiting the Doctor's return.]

VASILY LEONIDITCH [to Peasants] And do you fatten pigs? There's a first-rate business!

FIRST PEASANT. That's just so. We do go in for the pig-fattening line now and then.

VASILY LEONIDITCH. This kind?... [Grunts like a pig].

ANNA PAVLOVNA. Vovo, Vovo, leave off!

VASILY LEONIDITCH. Isn't it like? Eh, what?

FIRST PEASANT. That's just so. It's very resemblant.

ANNA PAVLOVNA. Vovo, leave off, I tell you!

SECOND PEASANT. What's it all about?

THIRD PEASANT. I said, we'd better go to some lodging meanwhile!

[Enter Doctor and Gregory.]

DOCTOR. What's the matter? What's happened?

ANNA PAVLOVNA. Why, you're always saying I must not get excited. Now, how is it possible to keep calm? I do not see my own sister for two months, and am careful about any doubtful visitor, and here are people from Koursk, straight from Koursk, where there is an epidemic of diphtheria, right in my house!

DOCTOR. These good fellows you mean, I suppose?

ANNA PAVLOVNA. Of course. Straight from a diphtheric place!

DOCTOR. Well, of course, if they come from an infected place it is rash; but still there is no reason to excite yourself so much about it.

ANNA PAVLOVNA. But don't you yourself advise carefulness?

DOCTOR. Of course, of course. Still, why excite yourself?

ANNA PAVLOVNA. How can I help it? Now we shall have to have the house completely disinfected.

DOCTOR. Oh no! Why completely? That would cost 300 roubles or more. I'll arrange it cheaply and well for you. Take, to a large bottle of water ...

ANNA PAVLOVNA. Boiled?

DOCTOR. It's all the same. Boiled would be better. To one bottle of water take a tablespoon of salicylic acid, and have everything they have come in contact with washed with the solution. As to the fellows themselves, they must be off, of course. That's all. Then you're quite safe. And it would do no harm to sprinkle some of the same solution through a spray, two or three tumblers, you'll see how well it will act. No danger whatever!

ANNA PAVLOVNA. Tanya! Where is Tanya?

[Enter Tanya.]

TANYA. Did you call, M'm?

ANNA PAVLOVNA. You know that big bottle in my dressing-room?

TANYA. Out of which we sprinkled the laundress yesterday?

ANNA PAVLOVNA. Well, of course! What other bottle could I mean? Well then, take that bottle and first wash with soap the place where they have been standing, and then with ...

TANYA. Yes, M'm; I know how.

ANNA PAVLOVNA. And then take the spray ... However, I had better do that myself when I get back.

DOCTOR. Well then, do so, and don't be afraid! Well, au revoir till this evening. [Exit].

ANNA PAVLOVNA. And they must be off! Not a trace of them must remain! Get out, get out! Go, what are you looking at?

FIRST PEASANT. That's just so. It's because of our stupidity, as we were instructed ...

GREGORY [pushes the Peasants out] There, there; be off!

SECOND PEASANT. Let me have my handkerchief back! [The handkerchief in which the presents were wrapped].

THIRD PEASANT. Oh Lord, oh Lord! didn't I say, some lodging-house meanwhile!

[Gregory pushes him out. Exeunt Peasants.]

PORTER [who has repeatedly tried to say something] Will there be any answer?

ANNA PAVLOVNA. Ah, from Bourdier? [Excitedly] None! None! You can take it back. I told her I never ordered such a costume, and I will not allow my daughter to wear it!

PORTER. I know nothing about it. I was sent ...

ANNA PAVLOVNA. Go, go, take it back! I will call myself about it!

VASILY LEONIDITCH [solemnly] Sir Messenger from Bourdier, depart!

PORTER. I might have been told that long ago. I have sat here nearly five hours!

VASILY LEONIDITCH. Ambassador from Bourdier, begone!

ANNA PAVLOVNA. Cease, please!

[Exit Porter.]

ANNA PAVLOVNA. Betsy! Where is she? I always have to wait for her.

VASILY LEONIDITCH [shouting at the top of his voice] Betsy! Petristchef! Come quick, quick, quick! Eh? What?

[Enter Petristchef, Betsy, and Marya Konstantinovna.]

ANNA PAVLOVNA. You always keep one waiting!

BETSY. On the contrary, I was waiting for you!

[Petristchef bows with his head only, then kisses Anna Pavlovna's hand.]

ANNA PAVLOVNA. How d'you do! [To Betsy] You always have an answer ready!

BETSY. If you are upset, mamma, I had better not go.

ANNA PAVLOVNA. Are we going or not?

BETSY. Well, let us go; it can't be helped.

ANNA PAVLOVNA. Did you see the man from Bourdier?

BETSY. Yes, and I was very glad. I ordered the costume, and am going to wear it when it is paid for.

ANNA PAVLOVNA. I am not going to pay for a costume that is indecent!

BETSY. Why has it become indecent? First it was decent, and now you have a fit of prudery.

ANNA PAVLOVNA. Not prudery at all! If the bodice were completely altered, then it would do.

BETSY. Mamma, that is quite impossible.

ANNA PAVLOVNA. Well, get dressed. [They sit down. Gregory puts on their over-shoes for them].

VASILY LEONIDITCH. Marya Konstantinovna, do you notice a vacuum in the hall?

MARYA KONSTANTINOVNA. What is it? [Laughs in anticipation].

VASILY LEONIDITCH. Bourdier's man has gone! Eh, what? Good, eh? [Laughs loudly].

ANNA PAVLOVNA. Well, let us go. [Goes out of the door, but returns at once] Tanya!

TANYA. Yes, M'm?

ANNA PAVLOVNA. Don't let Frisk catch cold while I am away. If she wants to be let out, put on her little yellow cloak. She is not quite well to-day.

TANYA. Yes, M'm.

[Exeunt Anna Pavlovna, Betsy, and Gregory.]

PETRISTCHEF. Well, have you got it?

VASILY LEONIDITCH. Not without trouble, I can tell you! First I rushed at the gov'nor; he began to bellow and turned me out. Off to the mater, I got it out of her. It's here! [Slaps his breast pocket] If once I make up my mind, there's no getting away from me. I have a deadly grip! Eh, what? And d'you know, my wolf-hounds are coming to-day.

[Petristchef and Vasily Leoniditch put on their outdoor things and go out. Tanya follows.]

THEODORE IVANITCH [alone] Yes, nothing but unpleasantness. How is it they can't live in peace? But one must say the new generation are not the thing. And as to the women's dominion!... Why, Leonid Fyodoritch just now was going to put in a word, but seeing what a frenzy she was in, slammed the door behind him. He is a wonderfully kind-hearted man. Yes, wonderfully kind. What's this? Here's Tanya bringing them back again!

TANYA. Come in, come in, grand-dads, never mind!

[Enter Tanya and the Peasants.]

THEODORE IVANITCH. Why have you brought them back?

TANYA. Well, Theodore Ivanitch, we must do something about their business. I shall have to wash the place anyhow.

THEODORE IVANITCH. But the business will not come off, I see that already.

FIRST PEASANT. How could we best put our affair into action, respected sir? Your reverence might take a little trouble over it, and we should give you full thankings from the Commune for your trouble.

THIRD PEASANT. Do try, honey! We can't live! We have so little land. Talk of cattle, why, we have no room to keep a hen! [They bow].

THEODORE IVANITCH. I am sorry for you, friends, but I can't think of any way to help you. I understand your case very well, but he has refused. So what can one do? Besides, the lady is also against it. Well, give me your papers, I'll try and see what I can do, but I hardly hope to succeed. [Exit].

[Tanya and the three Peasants sigh.]

TANYA. But tell me, grand-dads, what is it that is wanted?

FIRST PEASANT. Why, only that he should put his signature to our document.

TANYA. That the master should sign? Is that all?

FIRST PEASANT. Yes, only lay his signature on the deed and take the money, and there would be an end of the matter.

THIRD PEASANT. He only has to write and sign, as the peasants, let's say, desire, so, let's say, I also desire. That's the whole affair, if he'd only take it and sign it, it's all done.

TANYA [considering] He need only sign the paper and it's done?

FIRST PEASANT. That's just so. The whole matter is in dependence on that, and nothing else. Let him sign, and we ask no more.

TANYA. Just wait and see what Theodore Ivanitch will say. If he cannot persuade the master, I'll try something.

FIRST PEASANT. Get round him, will you?

TANYA. I'll try.

THIRD PEASANT. Ay, the lass is going to bestir herself. Only get the thing settled, and the Commune will bind itself to keep you all your life. See there, now!

FIRST PEASANT. If the affair can be put into action, truly we might put her in a gold frame.

SECOND PEASANT. That goes without saying!

TANYA. I can't promise for certain, but as the saying is: "An attempt is no sin, if you try …"

FIRST PEASANT. "You may win." That's just so.

[Enter Theodore Ivanitch.]

THEODORE IVANITCH. No, friends, it's no go! He has not done it, and he won't do it. Here, take your document. You may go.

FIRST PEASANT [gives Tanya the paper] Then it's on you we pin all our reliance, for example.

TANYA. Yes, yes! You go into the street, and I'll run out to you in a minute and have a word with you.

[Exeunt Peasants.]

TANYA. Theodore Ivanitch, dear Theodore Ivanitch, ask the master to come out and speak to me for a moment. I have something to say to him.

THEODORE IVANITCH. What next?

TANYA. I must, Theodore Ivanitch. Ask him, do; there's nothing wrong about it, on my sacred word.

THEODORE IVANITCH. But what do you want with him?

TANYA. That's a little secret. I will tell you later on, only ask him.

THEODORE IVANITCH [smiling] I can't think what you are up to! All right, I'll go and ask him. [Exit].

TANYA. I'll do it! Didn't he say himself that there is that power in Simon? And I know how to manage. No one found me out that time, and now I'll teach Simon what to do. If it doesn't succeed it's no great matter. After all it's not a sin.

[Enter Leonid Fyodoritch followed by Theodore Ivanitch.]

LEONID FYODORITCH [smiling] Is this the petitioner? Well, what is your business?

TANYA. It's a little secret, Leonid Fyodoritch; let me tell it you alone.

LEONID FYODORITCH. What is it? Theodore, leave us for a minute.

[Exit Theodore Ivanitch.]

TANYA. As I have grown up and lived in your house, Leonid Fyodoritch, and as I am very grateful to you for everything, I shall open my heart to you as to a father. Simon, who is living in your house, wants to marry me.

LEONID FYODORITCH. So that's it!

TANYA. I open my heart to you as to a father! I have no one to advise me, being an orphan.

LEONID FYODORITCH. Well, and why not? He seems a nice lad.

TANYA. Yes, that's true. He would be all right; there is only one thing I have my doubts about. It's something about him that I have noticed and can't make out ... perhaps it is something bad.

LEONID FYODORITCH. What is it? Does he drink?

TANYA. God forbid! But since I know that there is such a thing as spiritalism ...

LEONID FYODORITCH. Ah, you know that?

TANYA. Of course! I understand it very well. Some, of course, through ignorance, don't understand it.

LEONID FYODORITCH. Well, what then?

TANYA. I am very much afraid for Simon. It does happen to him.

LEONID FYODORITCH. What happens to him?

TANYA. Something of a kind like spiritalism. You ask any of the servants. As soon as he gets drowsy at the table, the table begins to tremble, and creak like that: tuke, ... tuke! All the servants have heard it.

LEONID FYODORITCH. Why, it's the very thing I was saying to Sergey Ivanitch this morning! Yes?...

TANYA. Or else ... when was it?... Oh yes, last Wednesday. We sat down to dinner, and the spoon just jumps into his hand of itself!

LEONID FYODORITCH. Ah, that is interesting! Jumps into his hand? When he was drowsing?

TANYA. That I didn't notice. I think he was, though.

LEONID FYODORITCH. Yes?...

TANYA. And that's what I'm afraid of, and what I wanted to ask you about. May not some harm come of it? To live one's life together, and him having such a thing in him!

LEONID FYODORITCH [smiling] No, you need not be afraid, there is nothing bad in that. It only proves him to be a medium, simply a medium. I knew him to be a medium before this.

TANYA. So that's what it is! And I was afraid!

LEONID FYODORITCH. No, there's nothing to be afraid of. [Aside]. That's capital! Kaptchitch can't come, so we will test him to-night.... [To Tanya] No, my dear, don't be afraid, he will be a good husband and ... that is only a kind of special power, and every one has it, only in some it is weaker and in others stronger.

TANYA. Thank you, sir. Now I shan't think any more about it; but I was so frightened.... What a thing it is, our want of education!

LEONID FYODORITCH. No, no, don't be frightened... Theodore!

[Enter Theodore Ivanitch.]

LEONID FYODORITCH. I am going out now. Get everything ready for to-night's seance.

THEODORE IVANITCH. But Mr. Kaptchitch is not coming.

LEONID FYODORITCH. That does not matter. [Puts on overcoat] We shall have a trial seance with our own medium. [Exit. Theodore Ivanitch goes out with him].

TANYA [alone] He believes it! He believes it! [Shrieks and jumps with joy] He really believes it! Isn't it wonderful! [Shrieks] Now I'll do it, if only Simon has pluck for it!

[Theodore Ivanitch returns.]

THEODORE IVANITCH. Well, have you told him your secret?

TANYA. I'll tell you too, only later on.... But I have a favour to ask of you too, Theodore Ivanitch.

THEODORE IVANITCH. Yes? What is it?

TANYA [shyly] You have been a second father to me, and I will open my heart before you as before God.

THEODORE IVANITCH. Don't beat about the bush, but come straight to the point.

TANYA. The point is ... well, the point is, that Simon wants to marry me.

THEODORE IVANITCH. Is that it? I thought I noticed ...

TANYA. Well, why should I hide it? I am an orphan, and you know yourself how matters are in these town establishments. Every one comes bothering; there's that Gregory Mihaylitch, for instance, he gives me no peace. And also that other one ... you know. They think I have no soul, and am only here for their amusement.

THEODORE IVANITCH. Good girl, that's right! Well, what then?

TANYA. Well, Simon wrote to his father; and he, his father, sees me to-day, and says: "He's spoilt" he means his son. Theodore Ivanitch [bows], take the place of a father to me, speak to the old man, to Simon's father! I could take them into the kitchen, and you might come in and speak to the old man!

THEODORE IVANITCH [smiling] Then I am to turn match-maker, am I? Well, I can do that.

TANYA. Theodore Ivanitch, dearest, be a father to me, and I'll pray for you all my life long.

THEODORE IVANITCH. All right, all right, I'll come later on. Haven't I promised? [Takes up newspaper].

TANYA. You are a second father to me!

THEODORE IVANITCH. All right, all right.

TANYA. Then I'll rely on you. [Exit].

THEODORE IVANITCH [alone, shaking his head] A good affectionate girl. To think that so many like her perish! Get but once into trouble and she'll go from hand to hand until she sinks into the mire, and can never be found again! There was that dear little Nataly. She, too, was a good girl, reared and cared for by a mother. [Takes up paper] Well, let's see what tricks Ferdinand is up to in Bulgaria.

[Curtain.]

ACT II

Evening of the same day. The scene represents the interior of the servants' kitchen. The Peasants have taken off their outer garments and sit drinking tea at the table, and perspiring. Theodore Ivanitch is smoking a cigar at the other side of the stage. The discharged Cook is lying on the brick oven, and is unseen during the early part of the scene.

THEODORE IVANITCH. My advice is, don't hinder him! If it's his wish and hers, in Heaven's name let him do it. She is a good, honest girl. Never mind her being a bit dressy; she can't help that, living in town: she is a good girl all the same.

SECOND PEASANT. Well, of course, if it is his wish, let him! He'll have to live with her, not me. But she's certainly uncommon spruce. How's one to take her into one's hut? Why, she'll not let her mother-in-law so much as pat her on the head.

THEODORE IVANITCH. That does not depend on the spruceness, but on character. If her nature is good, she's sure to be docile and respectful.

SECOND PEASANT. Ah, well, we'll have her if the lad's bent on having her. After all, it's a bad job to live with one as one don't care for. I'll consult my missus, and then may Heaven bless them!

THEODORE IVANITCH. Then let's shake hands on it!

SECOND PEASANT. Well, it seems it will have to come off.

FIRST PEASANT. Eh, Zachary! fortune's a-smiling on you! You've come to accomplish a piece of business, and just see what a duchess of a daughter-in-law you've obtained. All that's left to be done is to have a drink on it, and then it will be all in order.

THEODORE IVANITCH. That's not at all necessary. [An awkward silence].

THEODORE IVANITCH. I know something of your way of life too, you know. I am even thinking of purchasing a bit of land, building a cottage, and working on the land myself somewhere: maybe in your neighbourhood.

SECOND PEASANT. A very good thing too.

FIRST PEASANT. That's just it. When one has got the money one can get all kinds of pleasure in the country.

THIRD PEASANT. Say no more about it! Country life, let's say, is freer in every way, not like the town!

THEODORE IVANITCH. There now, would you let me join your Commune if I settled among you?

SECOND PEASANT. Why not? If you stand drink for the Elders, they'll accept you soon enough!

FIRST PEASANT. And if you open a public-house, for example, or an inn, why, you'd have such a life you'd never need to die! You might live like a king, and no mistake.

THEODORE IVANITCH. Well, we'll see. I should certainly like to have a few quiet years in my old age. Though my life here is good enough, and I should be sorry to leave. Leonid Fyodoritch is an exceedingly kind-hearted man.

FIRST PEASANT. That's just it. But how about our business? Is it possible that he is going to leave it without any termination?

THEODORE IVANITCH. He'd do it willingly.

SECOND PEASANT. It seems he's afraid of his wife.

THEODORE IVANITCH. It's not that he's afraid, but they don't hit things off together.

THIRD PEASANT. But you should try, father! How are we to live else? We've so little land ...

THEODORE IVANITCH. We'll see what comes of Tanya's attempt. She's taken the business into her hands now!

THIRD PEASANT [takes a sip of tea] Father, be merciful. We've so little land. A hen, let's say, we've no room for a hen, let alone the cattle.

THEODORE IVANITCH. If the business depended on me.... [To Second Peasant] Well, friend, so we've done our bit of match-making! It's agreed then about Tanya?

SECOND PEASANT. I've given my word, and I'll not go back on it without a good reason. If only our business succeeds!

[Enter Servants' Cook who looks up at the oven, makes a sign, and then begins to speak animatedly to Theodore Ivanitch.]

SERVANTS' COOK. Just now Simon was called upstairs from the front kitchen! The master and that other bald-headed one who calls up spirits with him, ordered him to sit down and take the place of Kaptchitch!

THEODORE IVANITCH. You don't say so!

SERVANTS' COOK. Yes, Jacob told Tanya.

THEODORE IVANITCH. Extraordinary!

[Enter Coachman.]

THEODORE IVANITCH. What do you want?

COACHMAN [to Theodore Ivanitch] You may just tell them I never agreed to live with a lot of dogs! Let any one who likes do it, but I will never agree to live among dogs!

THEODORE IVANITCH. What dogs?

COACHMAN. Three dogs have been sent into our room by Vasily Leoniditch! They've messed it all over. They're whining, and if one comes near them they bite, the devils! They'd tear you to pieces if you didn't mind. I've a good mind to take a club and smash their legs for them!

THEODORE IVANITCH. But when did they come?

COACHMAN. Why, to-day, from the Dog Show; the devil knows what kind they are, but they're an expensive sort. Are we or the dogs to live in the coachmen's quarters? You just go and ask!

THEODORE IVANITCH. Yes, that will never do. I'll go and ask about it.

COACHMAN. They'd better be brought here to Loukerya.

SERVANTS' COOK [angrily] People have to eat here, and you'd like to lock dogs in here! As it is ...

COACHMAN. And I've got the liveries, and the sledge-covers and the harness there, and they expect things kept clean! Perhaps the porter's lodge might do.

THEODORE IVANITCH. I must ask Vasily Leoniditch.

COACHMAN [angrily] He'd better hang the brutes round his neck and lug them about with him! But no fear: he'd rather ride on horseback himself. It's he as spoilt Beauty without rhyme or reason. That was a horse!... Oh dear! what a life! [Exit, slamming door].

THEODORE IVANITCH. That's not right! Certainly not right! [To Peasants] Well then, it's time we were saying good-bye, friends.

PEASANTS. Good-bye!

[Exit Theodore Ivanitch.]

[As soon as he is gone a sound of groaning is heard from the top of the oven.]

SECOND PEASANT. He's sleek, that one; looks like a general.

SERVANTS' COOK. Rather! Why, he has a room all to himself; he gets his washing, his tea and sugar, and food from the master's table.

DISCHARGED COOK [on the oven]. Why shouldn't the old beggar live well? He's lined his pockets all right!

SECOND PEASANT. Who's that up there, on the oven?

SERVANTS' COOK. Oh, it's only a man.

[Silence.]

FIRST PEASANT. Well, and you too, as I noticed a while since when you were supping, have capital food to eat.

SERVANTS' COOK. We can't complain. She's not mean about the food. We have wheat bread every Sunday, and fish when a holiday happens to be a fast-day too, and those who like may eat meat.

SECOND PEASANT. And does any one tuck into flesh on fast-days?

SERVANTS' COOK. Oh, they nearly all do! Only the old coachman, not the one who was here just now but the old one, and Simon, and I and the housekeeper, fast, all the others eat meat.

SECOND PEASANT. And the master himself?

SERVANTS' COOK. Catch him! Why, I bet he's forgotten there is such a thing as fasting!

THIRD PEASANT. Oh Lord!

FIRST PEASANT. That's the gentlefolks' way: they have got it all out of their books. 'Cos of their intelex!

THIRD PEASANT. Shouldn't wonder if they feed on wheat bread every day!

SERVANTS' COOK. Wheat bread indeed! Much they think of wheat bread! You should see what food they eat. No end of different things!

FIRST PEASANT. In course gentlefolks' food is of an airial kind.

SERVANTS' COOK. Airial, of course, but all the same they're good at stuffing themselves, they are!

FIRST PEASANT. Have healthy appekites, so to say.

SERVANTS' COOK. 'Cos they always rinse it down! All with sweet wines, and spirits, and fizzy liquors. They have a different one to suit every kind of food. They eat and rinse it down, and eat and rinse it down, they do.

FIRST PEASANT. And so the food's floated down in proportion, so to say.

SERVANTS' COOK. Ah yes, they are good at stuffing! It's awful! You see, it's not just sitting down, eating, then saying grace and going away, they're always at it!

SECOND PEASANT. Like pigs with their feet in the trough! [Peasants laugh].

SERVANTS' COOK. As soon as, by God's grace, they have opened their eyes, the samovar is brought in, tea, coffee, chocolate. Hardly is the second samovar emptied, a third has to be set. Then lunch, then dinner, then again coffee. They've hardly left off, then comes tea, and all sorts of tit-bits and sweetmeats, there's never an end to it! They even lie in bed and eat!

THIRD PEASANT. There now; that's good! [Laughs].

FIRST AND SECOND PEASANTS. What are you about?

THIRD PEASANT. If I could only live a single day like that!

SECOND PEASANT. But when do they do their work?

SERVANTS' COOK. Work indeed! What is their work? Cards and piano, that's all their work. The young lady used to sit down to the piano as soon as she opened her eyes, and off she'd go! And that other one who lives here, the teacher, stands and waits. "When will the piano be free?" When one has finished, off rattles the other, and sometimes they'd put two pianos near one another and four of 'em would bust out at once. Bust out in such a manner, you could hear 'em down here!

THIRD PEASANT. Oh Lord!

SERVANTS' COOK. Well, and that's all the work they do! Piano or cards! As soon as they have met together, cards, wine, smoking, and so on all night long. And as soon as they are up: eating again!

[Enter Simon.]

SIMON. Hope you're enjoying your tea!

FIRST PEASANT. Come and join us.

SIMON [comes up to the table] Thank you kindly. [First Peasant pours out a cup of tea for him].

SECOND PEASANT. Where have you been?

SIMON. Upstairs.

SECOND PEASANT. Well, and what was being done there?

SIMON. Why, I couldn't make it out at all! I don't know how to explain it.

SECOND PEASANT. But what was it?

SIMON. I can't explain it. They have been trying some kind of strength in me. I can't make it out. Tanya says, "Do it, and we'll get the land for our peasants; he'll sell it them."

SECOND PEASANT. But how is she going to manage it?

SIMON. I can't make it out, and she won't say. She says, "Do as I tell you," and that's all.

SECOND PEASANT. But what is it you have to do?

SIMON. Nothing just now. They made me sit down, put out the lights and told me to sleep. And Tanya had hidden herself there. They didn't see her, but I did.

SECOND PEASANT. Why? What for?

SIMON. The Lord only knows, I can't make it out.

FIRST PEASANT. Naturally it is for the distraction of time.

SECOND PEASANT. Well, it's clear you and I can make nothing of it. You had better tell me whether you have taken all your wages yet.

SIMON. No, I've not drawn any. I have twenty-eight roubles to the good, I think.

SECOND PEASANT. That's all right! Well, if God grants that we get the land, I'll take you home, Simon.

SIMON. With all my heart!

SECOND PEASANT. You've got spoilt, I should say. You'll not want to plough?

SIMON. Plough? Only give me the chance! Plough or mow, I'm game. Those are things one doesn't forget.

FIRST PEASANT. But it don't seem very desirous after town life, for example? Eh!

SIMON. It's good enough for me. One can live in the country too.

FIRST PEASANT. And Daddy Mitry here, is already on the look-out for your place; he's hankering after a life of luckshury!

SIMON. Eh, Daddy Mitry, you'd soon get sick of it. It seems easy enough when one looks at it, but there's a lot of running about that takes it out of one.

SERVANTS' COOK. You should see one of their balls, Daddy Mitry, then you would be surprised!

THIRD PEASANT. Why, do they eat all the time?

SERVANTS' COOK. My eye! You should have seen what we had here awhile ago. Theodore Ivanitch took me upstairs and I peeped in. The ladies, awful! Dressed up! Dressed up, bless my heart, and all bare down to here, and their arms bare.

THIRD PEASANT. Oh Lord!

SECOND PEASANT. Faugh! How beastly!

FIRST PEASANT. I take it the climate allows of that sort of thing!

SERVANTS' COOK. Well, daddy, so I peeped in. Dear me, what it was like! All of 'em in their natural skins! Would you believe it: old women, our mistress, only think, she's a grandmother, and even she'd gone and bared her shoulders.

THIRD PEASANT. Oh Lord!

SERVANTS' COOK. And what next? The music strikes up, and each man of 'em went up to his own, catches hold of her, and off they go twirling round and round!

SECOND PEASANT. The old women too?

SERVANTS' COOK. Yes, the old ones too.

SIMON. No, the old ones sit still.

SERVANTS' COOK. Get along, I've seen it myself!

SIMON. No they don't.

DISCHARGED COOK [in a hoarse voice, looking down from the oven] That's the Polka-Mazurka. You fools don't understand what dancing is. The way they dance ...

SERVANTS' COOK. Shut up, you dancer! And keep quiet, there's some one coming.

[Enter Gregory; old Cook hides hurriedly.]

GREGORY [to Servants' Cook] Bring some sour cabbage.

SERVANTS' COOK. I am only just up from the cellar, and now I must go down again! Who is it for?

GREGORY. For the young ladies. Be quick, and send it up with Simon. I can't wait!

SERVANTS' COOK. There now, they tuck into sweetmeats till they are full up, and then they crave for sour cabbage!

FIRST PEASANT. That's to make a clearance.

SERVANTS' COOK. Of course, and as soon as there is room inside, they begin again! [Takes basin, and exit].

GREGORY [at Peasants] Look at them, how they've established themselves down here! Mind, if the mistress finds it out she'll give it you hot, like she did this morning! [Exit, laughing].

FIRST PEASANT. That's just it, she did raise a storm that time, awful!

SECOND PEASANT. That time it looked as if the master was going to step in, but seeing that the missus was about to blow the very roof off the house, he slams the door. Have your own way, thinks he.

THIRD PEASANT [waving his arm] It's the same everywhere. My old woman, let's say, she kicks up such a rumpus sometimes, it's just awful! Then I just get out of the hut. Let her go to Jericho! She'll give you one with the poker if you don't mind. Oh Lord!

[Jacob enters hurriedly with a prescription.]

JACOB. Here, Simon, you run to the chemist's and get these powders for the mistress!

SIMON. But master told me not to go out.

JACOB. You've plenty of time; your business won't begin till after their tea. Hope you are enjoying your tea!

FIRST PEASANT. Thanks, come and join us.

[Exit Simon.]

JACOB. I haven't time. However, I'll just have one cup for company's sake.

FIRST PEASANT. And we've just been having a conversation as to how your mistress carried on so haughty this morning.

JACOB. Oh, she's a reg'lar fury! So hot-tempered, that she gets quite beside herself. Sometimes she even bursts out crying.

FIRST PEASANT. Now, there's a thing I wanted to ask you about. What, for example, be these mikerots she was illuding to erewhile? "They've infested the house with mikerots, with mikerots," she says. What is one to make of these same mikerots?

JACOB. Mikerogues, you mean! Well, it seems there is such a kind of bugs; all illnesses come from them, they say. So she says there are some of 'em on you. After you were gone, they washed and washed and sprinkled the place where you had stood. There's a kind of physic as kills these same bugs, they say.

SECOND PEASANT. Then where have we got these bugs on us?

JACOB [drinking his tea] Why, they say they're so small that one can't see 'em even through a glass.

SECOND PEASANT. Then how does she know I've got 'em on me? Perhaps there's more of that muck on her than on me!

JACOB. There now, you go and ask her!

SECOND PEASANT. I believe it's humbug.

JACOB. Of course it's bosh. The doctors must invent something, or else what are they paid for? There's one comes to us every day. Comes, talks a bit, and pockets ten roubles!

SECOND PEASANT. Nonsense!

JACOB. Why, there's one as takes a hundred!

FIRST PEASANT. A hundred? Humbug!

JACOB. A hundred. Humbug, you say? Why, if he has to go out of town, he'll not do it for less than a thousand! "Give a thousand," he says, "or else you may kick the bucket for what I care!"

THIRD PEASANT. Oh Lord!

SECOND PEASANT. Then does he know some charm?

JACOB. I suppose he must. I served at a General's outside Moscow once: a cross, terrible proud old fellow he was, just awful. Well, this General's daughter fell ill. They send for that doctor at once. "A thousand roubles, then I'll come." Well, they agreed, and he came. Then they did something or other he didn't like, and he bawled out at the General and says, "Is this the way you show your respect for me? Then I'll not attend her!" And, oh my! The old General forgot all his pride, and starts wheedling him in every way not to chuck up the job!

FIRST PEASANT. And he got the thousand?

JACOB. Of course!

SECOND PEASANT. That's easy got money. What wouldn't a peasant do with such a sum!

THIRD PEASANT. And I think it's all bosh. That time my foot was festering I had it doctored ever so long. I spent nigh on five roubles on it, then I gave up doctoring, and it got all right!

[Discharged Cook on the oven coughs.]

JACOB. Ah, the old crony is here again!

FIRST PEASANT. Who might that man be?

JACOB. He used to be our master's cook. He comes to see Loukerya.

FIRST PEASANT. Kitchen-master, as one might say. Then, does he live here?

JACOB. No, they won't allow that. He's here one day, there another. If he's got a copper he goes to a dosshouse; but when he has drunk all, he comes here.

SECOND PEASANT. How did he come to this?

JACOB. Simply grew weak. And what a man he used to be like a gentleman! Went about with a gold watch; got forty roubles a month wages. And now look at him! He'd have starved to death long ago if it hadn't been for Loukerya.

[Enter Servants' Cook with the sour cabbage.]

JACOB [to Servants' Cook] I see you've got Paul Petrovitch here again?

SERVANTS' COOK. And where's he to go to? Is he to go and freeze?

THIRD PEASANT. What liquor does.... Liquor, let's say ... [Clicks his tongue sympathetically].

SECOND PEASANT. Of course. A firm man's firm as a rock; a weak man's weaker than water.

DISCHARGED COOK [gets off the oven with trembling hands and legs] Loukerya, I say, give us a drop!

SERVANTS' COOK. What are you up to? I'll give you such a drop!...

DISCHARGED COOK. Have you no conscience? I'm dying! Brothers, a copper ...

SERVANTS' COOK. Get back on the oven, I tell you!

DISCHARGED COOK. Half a glass only, cook, for Heaven's sake! I say, do you understand? I ask you in the name of Heaven, now!

SERVANTS' COOK. Come along, here's some tea for you.

DISCHARGED COOK. Tea; what is tea? Weak, sloppy stuff. A little vodka, just one little drop ... Loukerya!

THIRD PEASANT. Poor old soul, what agony it is!

SECOND PEASANT. You'd better give him some.

SERVANTS' COOK [gets out a bottle and fills a wine-glass] Here you are; you'll get no more.

DISCHARGED COOK [clutches hold of it and drinks, trembling all over] Loukerya, Cook! I am drinking, and you must understand ...

SERVANTS' COOK. Now then, stop your chatter! Get on to the oven, and let not a breath of you be heard! [The old Cook meekly begins to climb up, muttering something to himself].

SECOND PEASANT. What it is, when a man gives way to his weakness!

FIRST PEASANT. That's just it, human weakness.

THIRD PEASANT. That goes without saying.

[The Discharged Cook settles down, muttering all the time. Silence.]

SECOND PEASANT. I want to ask you something: that girl of Aksinya's as comes from our village and is living here. How is she? What is she like? How is she living, I mean, does she live honest?

JACOB. She's a nice girl; one can say nothing but good of her.

SERVANTS' COOK. I'll tell you straight, daddy; I know this here establishment out and out, and if you mean to have Tanya for your son's wife, be quick about it, before she comes to grief, or else she'll not escape!

JACOB. Yes, that's true. A while ago we had a girl here, Nataly. She was a good girl too. And she was lost without rhyme or reason. No better than that chap! [Pointing to the old Cook].

SERVANTS' COOK. There's enough to dam a mill-pool, with the likes of us, as perish! 'Cos why, every one is tempted by the easy life and the good food. And see there, as soon as one has tasted the good food she goes and slips. And once she's slipped, they don't want her, but get a fresh one in her place.

So it was with dear little Nataly; she also slipped, and they turned her out. She had a child and fell ill, and died in the hospital last spring. And what a girl she used to be!

THIRD PEASANT. Oh Lord! People are weak; they ought to be pitied.

DISCHARGED COOK. Those devils pity? No fear! [He hangs his legs down from the oven] I have stood roasting myself by the kitchen range for thirty years, and now that I am not wanted, I may go and die like a dog.... Pity indeed!...

FIRST PEASANT. That's just it. It's the old circumstances.

SECOND PEASANT.
While they drank and they fed, you were "curly head."
When they'd finished the prog, 'twas "Get out, mangy dog!"

THIRD PEASANT. Oh Lord!

DISCHARGED COOK. Much you know. What is "Sautey a la Bongmont"? What is "Bavassary"? Oh, the things I could make! Think of it! The Emperor tasted my work, and now the devils want me no longer. But I am not going to stand it!

SERVANTS' COOK. Now then, stop that noise, mind.... Get up right into the corner, so that no one can see you, or else Theodore Ivanitch or some one may come in, and both you and me'll be turned out! [Silence].

JACOB. And do you know my part of the country? I'm from Voznesensky.

SECOND PEASANT. Not know it? Why, it's no more'n ten miles from our village; not that across the ford! Do you cultivate any land there?

JACOB. My brother does, and I send my wages. Though I live here, I am dying for a sight of home.

FIRST PEASANT. That's just it.

SECOND PEASANT. Then Anisim is your brother?

JACOB. Own brother. He lives at the farther end of the village.

SECOND PEASANT. Of course, I know; his is the third house.

[Enter Tanya, running.]

TANYA. Jacob, what are you doing, amusing yourself here? She is calling you!

JACOB. I'm coming; but what's up?

TANYA. Frisk is barking; it's hungry. And she's scolding you. "How cruel he is," she says. "He's no feeling," she says. "It's long past Frisk's dinner-time, and he has not brought her food!" [Laughs].

JACOB [rises to go] Oh, she's cross? What's going to happen now, I wonder?

SERVANTS' COOK. Here, take the cabbage with you.

JACOB. All right, give it here. [Takes basin, and exit].

FIRST PEASANT. Who is going to dine now?

TANYA. Why, the dog! It's her dog. [Sits down and takes up the tea-pot] Is there any more tea? I've brought some. [Puts fresh tea into the tea-pot.]

FIRST PEASANT. Dinner for a dog?

TANYA. Yes, of course! They prepare a special cutlet for her; it must not be too fat. And I do the washing, the dog's washing, I mean.

THIRD PEASANT. Oh Lord!

TANYA. It's like that gentleman who had a funeral for his dog.

SECOND PEASANT. What's that?

TANYA. Why, some one told me he had a dog, I mean the gentleman had a dog. And it died. It was winter, and he went in his sledge to bury that dog. Well, he buried it, and on the way home he sits and cries, the gentleman does. Well, there was such a bitter frost that the coachman's nose keeps running, and he has to keep wiping it. Let me fill your cup! [Fills it] So he keeps wiping his nose, and the gentleman sees it, and says, "What are you crying about?" And the coachman, he says, "Why, sir, how can I help it; is there another dog like him?" [Laughs].

SECOND PEASANT. And I daresay he thinks to himself, "If your own self was to kick the bucket I'd not cry." [Laughs].

DISCHARGED COOK [from up on the oven] That is true; that's right!

TANYA. Well, the gentleman, he gets home and goes straight to his lady: "What a good-hearted man our coachman is; he was crying all the way home about poor Dash. Have him called.... Here, drink this glass of vodka," he says, "and here's a rouble as a reward for you." That's just like her saying Jacob has no feelings for her dog! [The Peasants laugh].

FIRST PEASANT. That's the style!

SECOND PEASANT. That was a go!

THIRD PEASANT. Ay, lassie, but you've set us a-laughing!

TANYA [pouring out more tea] Have some more! Yes, it only seems that our life is pleasant; but sometimes it is very disgusting, clearing up all their messes! Faugh! It's better in the country. [Peasants turn their cups upside-down, as a polite sign that they have had enough. Tanya pours out more tea] Have some more, Efim Antonitch. I'll fill your cup, Mitry Vlasitch.

THIRD PEASANT. All right, fill it, fill it.

FIRST PEASANT. Well, dear, and what progression is our business making?

TANYA. It's getting on ...

FIRST PEASANT: Well, dear, and what progression is our business making?

TANYA. It's getting on ...]

FIRST PEASANT. Simon told us ...

TANYA [quickly] Did he?

SECOND PEASANT. But he could not make us understand.

TANYA. I can't tell you now, but I'm doing my best, all I can! And I've got your paper here! [Shows the paper hidden under the bib of her apron] If only one thing succeeds.... [Shrieks] Oh, how nice it would be!

SECOND PEASANT. Don't lose that paper, mind. It has cost money.

TANYA. Never fear. You only want him to sign it? Is that all?

THIRD PEASANT. Why, what else? Let's say he's signed it, and it's done! [Turns his cup upside-down] I've had enough.

TANYA [aside] He'll sign it; you'll see he will... Have some more. [Pours out tea].

FIRST PEASANT. If only you get this business about the sale of the land settled, the Commune would pay your marriage expenses. [Refuses the tea].

TANYA [pouring out tea] Do have another cup.

THIRD PEASANT. You get it done, and we'll arrange your marriage, and I myself, let's say, will dance at the wedding. Though I've never danced in all my born days, I'll dance then!

TANYA [laughing] All right, I'll be in hopes of it. [Silence].

SECOND PEASANT [examines Tanya] That's all very well, but you're not fit for peasant work.

TANYA. Who? I? Why, don't you think me strong enough? You should see me lacing up my mistress. There's many a peasant couldn't tug as hard.

SECOND PEASANT. Where do you tug her to?

TANYA. Well, there's a thing made with bone, like, something like a stiff jacket, only up to here! Well, and I pull the strings just as when you saddle a horse, when you ... what d'ye call it? You know, when you spit on your hands!

SECOND PEASANT. Tighten the girths, you mean.

TANYA. Yes, yes, that's it. And you know I mustn't shove against her with my knee. [Laughs].

SECOND PEASANT. Why do you pull her in?

TANYA. For a reason!

SECOND PEASANT. Why, is she doing penance?

TANYA. No, it's for beauty's sake!

FIRST PEASANT. That's to say, you pull in her paunch for appearance' sake.

TANYA. Sometimes I lace her up so that her eyes are ready to start from her head, and she says, "Tighter," till my hands tingle. And you say I'm not strong! [Peasants laugh and shake their heads].

TANYA. But here, I've been jabbering. [Runs away, laughing].

THIRD PEASANT. Ah, the lassie has made us laugh!

FIRST PEASANT. She's a tidy one!

SECOND PEASANT. She's not bad.

[Enter Sahatof and Vasily Leoniditch. Sahatof holds a teaspoon in his hand.]

VASILY LEONIDITCH. Not exactly a dinner, but a dejeuner dinatoire. And first-rate it was, I tell you. Ham of sucking-pig, delicious! Roulier feeds one splendidly! I've only just returned. [Sees Peasants] Ah, the peasants are here again!

SAHATOF. Yes, yes, that's all very well, but we came here to hide this article. Where shall we hide it?

VASILY LEONIDITCH. Excuse me a moment. [To Servants' Cook] Where are the dogs?

SERVANTS' COOK. In the coachman's quarters. You can't keep dogs in the servants' kitchen!

VASILY LEONIDITCH. Ah, in the coachman's quarters? All right.

SAHATOF. I am waiting.

VASILY LEONIDITCH. Excuse me, please. Eh, what? Hide it? I'll tell you what. Let's put it into one of the peasants' pockets. That one. I say, where's your pocket? Eh, what?

THIRD PEASANT. What for d'ye want my pocket? You're a good 'un! My pocket! There's money in my pocket!

VASILY LEONIDITCH. Where's your bag, then?

THIRD PEASANT. What for?

SERVANTS' COOK. What d'you mean? That's the young master!

VASILY LEONIDITCH [laughs. To Sahatof] D'you know why he's so frightened? Shall I tell you? He's got a heap of money. Eh, what?

SAHATOF. Yes, yes, I see. Well, you talk to them a bit, and I'll put it into that bag without being observed, so that they should not notice and could not point it out to him. Talk to them.

VASILY LEONIDITCH. All right! [To Peasants] Well then, old fellows, how about the land? Are you buying it? Eh, what?

FIRST PEASANT. We have made an offering, so to say, with our whole heart. But there, the business don't come into action nohow.

VASILY LEONIDITCH. You should not be so stingy! Land is an important matter! I told you about planting mint. Or else tobacco would also do.

FIRST PEASANT. That's just it. Every kind of producks.

THIRD PEASANT. And you help us, master. Ask your father. Or else how are we to live? There's so little land. A fowl, let's say, there's not enough room for a fowl to run about.

SAHATOF [having put the spoon into a bag belonging to the Third Peasant] C'est fait. Ready. Come along. [Exit].

VASILY LEONIDITCH. So don't be stingy! Eh? Well, good-bye. [Exit].

THIRD PEASANT. Didn't I say, come to some lodging-house? Well, supposing we'd had to give three-pence each, then at least we'd have been in peace. As to here, the Lord be merciful! "Give us the money," he says. What's that for?

SECOND PEASANT. He's drunk, I daresay.

[Peasants turn their cups upside-down, rise, and cross themselves.]

FIRST PEASANT. And d'you mind what a saying he threw out? Sowing mint! One must know how to understand them, that one must!

SECOND PEASANT. Sow mint indeed! He'd better bend his own back at that work, and then it's not mint he'll hanker after, no fear! Well, many thanks!... And now, good woman, would you tell us where we could lie down to sleep?

SERVANTS' COOK. One of you can lie on the oven, and the others on these benches.

THIRD PEASANT. Christ save you! [Prays, crossing himself].

FIRST PEASANT. If only by God's help we get our business settled! [Lies down] Then to-morrow, after dinner, we'd be off by the train, and on Tuesday we'd be home again.

SECOND PEASANT. Are you going to put out the light?

SERVANTS' COOK. Put it out? Oh no! They'll keep running down here, first for one thing then another.... You lie down, I'll lower it.

SECOND PEASANT. How is one to live, having so little land? Why, this year, I have had to buy corn since Christmas. And the oat-straw is all used up. I'd like to get hold of ten acres, and then I could take Simon back.

THIRD PEASANT. You're a man with a family. You'd get the land cultivated without trouble. If only the business comes off.

SECOND PEASANT. We must pray to the Holy Virgin, maybe she'll help us out. [Silence, broken by sighs. Then footsteps and voices are heard outside. The door opens. Enter Grossman hurriedly, with his eyes bandaged, holding Sahatof's hand, and followed by the Professor and the Doctor, the Fat Lady and Leonid Fyodoritch, Betsy and Petristchef, Vasily Leoniditch and Marya Konstantinovna, Anna Pavlovna and the Baroness, Theodore Ivanitch and Tanya].

[Peasants jump up. Grossman comes forward stepping quickly, then stops.]

FAT LADY. You need not trouble yourselves; I have undertaken the task of observing, and am strictly fulfilling my duty! Mr. Sahatof, are you not leading him?

SAHATOF. Of course not!

FAT LADY. You must not lead him, but neither must you resist! [To Leonid Fyodoritch] I know these experiments. I have tried them myself. Sometimes I used to feel a certain effluence, and as soon as I felt it ...

LEONID FYODORITCH. May I beg of you to keep perfect silence?

FAT LADY. Oh, I understand so well! I have experienced it myself. As soon as my attention was diverted I could no longer ...

LEONID FYODORITCH. Sh ...!

[Grossman goes about, searches near the First and Second Peasants, then approaches the Third, and stumbles over a bench.]

BARONESS. Mais dites-moi, on le paye?[6]

ANNA PAVLOVNA. Je ne saurais vous dire.

[Note 6: BARONESS. But tell me, please, is he paid for this?]

ANNA PAVLOVNA. I really do not know.

BARONESS. Mais c'est un monsieur?[7]

ANNA PAVLOVNA. Oh, oui!

BARONESS. Ca tient du miraculeux. N'est ce pas? Comment est-ce qu'il trouve?

ANNA PAVLOVNA. Je ne saurais vous dire. Mon mari vous l'expliquera. [Noticing Peasants, turns round, and sees the Servants' Cook] Pardon ... what is this?

[Note 7: BARONESS. But he is a gentleman?]

ANNA PAVLOVNA. Oh yes!

BARONESS. It is almost miraculous. Isn't it? How does he manage to find things?

ANNA PAVLOVNA. I really can't tell you. My husband will explain it to you.... Excuse me....

[Baroness goes up to the group.]

ANNA PAVLOVNA [to Servants' Cook] Who let the peasants in?

SERVANTS' COOK. Jacob brought them in.

ANNA PAVLOVNA. Who gave Jacob the order?

SERVANTS' COOK. I can't say. Theodore Ivanitch has seen them.

ANNA PAVLOVNA. Leonid!

[Leonid Fyodoritch does not hear, being absorbed in the search, and says, Sh ...]

ANNA PAVLOVNA. Theodore Ivanitch! What is the meaning of this? Did you not see me disinfecting the whole hall, and now the whole kitchen is infected, all the rye bread, the milk ...

THEODORE IVANITCH. I thought there would not be any danger if they came here. The men have come on business. They have far to go, and are from our village.

ANNA PAVLOVNA. That's the worst of it! They are from the Koursk village, where people are dying of diphtheria like flies! But the chief thing is, I ordered them out of the house!... Did I, or did I not? [Approaches the others that have gathered round the Peasants] Be careful! Don't touch them, they are all infected with diphtheria! [No one heeds her, and she steps aside in a dignified manner and stands quietly waiting].

PETRISTCHEF [sniffs loudly] I don't know if it is diphtheria, but there is some kind of infection in the air. Don't you notice it?

BETSY. Stop your nonsense! Vovo, which bag is it in?

VASILY LEONIDITCH. That one, that one. He is getting near, very near!

PETRISTCHEF. Is it spirits divine, or spirits of wine?

BETSY. Now your cigarette comes in handy for once. Smoke closer, closer to me.

[Petristchef leans over her and smokes at her.]

VASILY LEONIDITCH. He's getting near, I tell you. Eh, what?

GROSSMAN [searches excitedly round the Third Peasant] It is here; I feel it is!

FAT LADY. Do you feel an effluence? [Grossman stoops and finds the spoon in the bag].

ALL. Bravo! [General enthusiasm].

VASILY LEONIDITCH. Ah! So that's where our spoon was. [To Peasants] Then that's the sort you are!

THIRD PEASANT. What sort? I didn't take your spoon! What are you making out? I didn't take it, and my soul knows nothing about it. I didn't take it, there! Let him do what he likes. I knew he came here for no good. "Where's your bag?" says he. I didn't take it, the Lord is my witness! [Crosses himself] I didn't take it!

[The young people group round the Peasant, laughing.]

LEONID FYODORITCH [angrily to his son] Always playing the fool! [To the Third Peasant] Never mind, friend! We know you did not take it; it was only an experiment.

GROSSMAN [removes bandage from his eyes, and pretends to be coming to] Can I have a little water? [All fuss round him].

VASILY LEONIDITCH. Let's go straight from here into the coachman's room. I've got a bitch there, epatante![8] Eh, what?

[Note 8: Stunning!]

BETSY. What a horrid word. Couldn't you say dog?

VASILY LEONIDITCH. No. I can't say, Betsy is a man, epatant. I should have to say young woman; it's a parallel case. Eh, what? Marya Konstantinovna, isn't it true? Good, eh? [Laughs loudly].

MARYA KONSTANTINOVNA. Well, let us go. [Exeunt Marya Konstantinovna, Betsy, Petristchef, and Vasily Leoniditch].

FAT LADY [to Grossman] Well? how are you? Have you rested? [Grossman does not answer. To Sahatof] And you, Mr. Sahatof, did you feel the effluence?

SAHATOF. I felt nothing. Yes, it was very fine, very fine. Quite a success!

BARONESS. Admirable! Ca ne le fait pas souffrir?[9]

LEONID FYODORITCH. Pas le moins du monde.

[Note 9: BARONESS. Capital! Does it not cause him any pain?]

LEONID FYODORITCH. Not the slightest.

PROFESSOR [to Grossman] May I trouble you? [Hands him a thermometer] At the beginning of the experiment it was 37 decimal 2, degrees.[10] [To Doctor] That's right, I think? Would you mind feeling his pulse? Some loss is inevitable.

[Note 10: He uses a Centigrade thermometer.]

DOCTOR [to Grossman] Now then, sir, let's have your hand; we'll see, we'll see. [Takes out his watch, and feels Grossman's pulse].

FAT LADY [to Grossman] One moment! The condition you were in could not be called sleep?

GROSSMAN [wearily] It was hypnosis.

SAHATOF. In that case, are we to understand that you hypnotised yourself?

GROSSMAN. And why not? An hypnotic state may ensue not only in consequence of association, the sound of the tom-tom, for instance, in Charcot's method, but by merely entering an hypnogenetic zone.

SAHATOF. Granting that, it would still be desirable to define what hypnotism is, more exactly?

PROFESSOR. Hypnotism is a phenomenon resulting from the transmutation of one energy into another.

GROSSMAN. Charcot does not so define it.

SAHATOF. A moment, just a moment! That is your definition, but Liebault told me himself ...

DOCTOR [lets go of Grossman's pulse] Ah, that's all right; well now, the temperature?

FAT LADY [interrupting] No, allow me! I agree with the Professor. And here's the very best proof. After my illness, when I lay insensible, a desire to speak came over me. In general I am of a silent disposition, but then I was overcome by this desire to speak, and I spoke and spoke, and I was told that I spoke in such a way that every one was astonished! [To Sahatof] But I think I interrupted you?

SAHATOF [with dignity] Not at all. Pray continue.

DOCTOR. Pulse 82, and the temperature has risen three-tenths of a degree.

PROFESSOR. There you are! That's a proof! That's just as it should be. [Takes out pocket-book and writes] 82, yes? And 37 and 5. When the hypnotic state is induced, it invariably produces a heightened action of the heart.

DOCTOR. I can, as a medical man, bear witness that your prognosis was justified by the event.

PROFESSOR [to Sahatof] You were saying?...

SAHATOF. I wished to say that Liebault told me himself that the hypnotic is only one particular psychical state, increasing susceptibility to suggestion.

PROFESSOR. That is so, but still the law of equivalents is the chief thing.

GROSSMAN. Moreover, Liebault is far from being an authority, while Charcot has studied the subject from all sides, and has proved that hypnotism produced by a blow, a trauma ...

All talking together.

{ SAHATOF. Yes, but I don't reject Charcot's labour. I know him also, I am only repeating what Liebault told me ...

{ GROSSMAN [excitedly] There are 3000 patients in the Salpetriere, and I have gone through the whole course.

{ PROFESSOR. Excuse me, gentlemen, but that is not the point.

FAT LADY [interrupting] One moment, I will explain it to you in two words? When my husband was ill, all the doctors gave him up ...

LEONID FYODORITCH. However, we had better go upstairs again. Baroness, this way!

[Exeunt Grossman, Sahatof, Professor, Doctor, the Fat Lady, and Baroness, talking loudly and interrupting each other.]

ANNA PAVLOVNA [catching hold of Leonid Fyodoritch's arm] How often have I asked you not to interfere in household matters! You think of nothing but your nonsense, and the whole house is on my shoulders. You will infect us all!

LEONID FYODORITCH. What? How? I don't understand what you mean.

ANNA PAVLOVNA. How? Why, people ill of diphtheria sleep in the kitchen, which is in constant communication with the whole house.

LEONID FYODORITCH. Yes, but I ...

ANNA PAVLOVNA. What, I?

LEONID FYODORITCH. I know nothing about it.

ANNA PAVLOVNA. It's your duty to know, if you are the head of the family. Such things must not be done.

LEONID FYODORITCH. But I never thought ... I thought ...

ANNA PAVLOVNA. It is sickening to listen to you! [Leonid Fyodoritch remains silent].

ANNA PAVLOVNA [to Theodore Ivanitch] Turn them out at once! They are to leave my kitchen immediately! It is terrible! No one listens to me; they do it out of spite.... I turn them out from there, and they bring them in here! And with my illness ... [Gets more and more excited, and at last begins to cry] Doctor! Doctor! Peter Petrovitch!... He's gone too!... [Exit, sobbing, followed by Leonid Fyodoritch].

[All stand silent for a long time.]

THIRD PEASANT. Botheration take them all! If one don't mind, the police will be after one here. And I have never been to law in all my born days. Let's go to some lodging-house, lads!

THEODORE IVANITCH [to Tanya] What are we to do?

TANYA. Never mind, Theodore Ivanitch, let them sleep with the coachman.

THEODORE IVANITCH. How can we do that? The coachman was complaining as it is, that his place is full of dogs.

TANYA. Well then, the porter's lodge.

THEODORE IVANITCH. And supposing it's found out?

TANYA. It won't be found out! Don't trouble about that, Theodore Ivanitch. How can one turn them out now, at night? They'll not find anywhere to go to.

THEODORE IVANITCH. Well, do as you please. Only they must go away from here. [Exit].

[Peasants take their bags.]

DISCHARGED COOK. Oh those damned fiends! It's all their fat! Fiends!

SERVANTS' COOK. You be quiet there. Thank goodness they didn't see you!

TANYA. Well then, daddy, come along to the porter's lodge.

FIRST PEASANT. Well, but how about our business? How, for example, about the applience of his hand to the signature? May we be in hopes?

TANYA. We'll see in an hour's time.

SECOND PEASANT. You'll do the trick?

TANYA [laughs] Yes, God willing!

[Curtain.]

ACT III
Evening of the same day. The small drawing-room in Leonid Fyodoritch's house, where the seances are always held. Leonid Fyodoritch and the Professor.

LEONID FYODORITCH. Well then, shall we risk a seance with our new medium?

PROFESSOR. Yes, certainly. He is a powerful medium, there is no doubt about it. And it is especially desirable that the seance should take place to-day with the same people. Grossman will certainly respond to the influence of the mediumistic energy, and then the connection and identity of the different phenomena will be still more evident. You will see then that, if the medium is as strong as he was just now, Grossman will vibrate.

LEONID FYODORITCH. Then I will send for Simon and ask those who wish to attend to come in.

PROFESSOR. Yes, all right! I will just jot down a few notes. [Takes out his note-book and writes].

[Enter Sahatof.]

SAHATOF. They have just settled down to whist in Anna Pavlovna's drawing-room, and as I am not wanted there and as I am interested in your séance, I have put in an appearance here. But will there be a seance?

LEONID FYODORITCH. Yes, certainly!

SAHATOF. In spite of the absence of Mr. Kaptchitch's mediumistic powers?

LEONID FYODORITCH. Vous avez la main heureuse.[11] Fancy, that very peasant whom I mentioned to you this morning, turns out to be an undoubted medium.

[Note 11: LEONID FYODORITCH. You bring good luck.]

SAHATOF. Dear me! Yes, that is peculiarly interesting!

LEONID FYODORITCH. Yes, we tried a few preliminary experiments with him just after dinner.

SAHATOF. So you've had time already to experiment, and to convince yourself ...

LEONID FYODORITCH. Yes, perfectly! And he turns out to be an exceptionally powerful medium.

SAHATOF [incredulously] Dear me!

LEONID FYODORITCH. It turns out that it has long been noticed in the servants' hall. When he sits down to table, the spoon springs into his hand of its own accord! [To the Professor] Had you heard about it?

PROFESSOR. No, I had not heard that detail.

SAHATOF [to the Professor]. But still, you admit the possibility of such phenomena?

PROFESSOR. What phenomena?

SAHATOF. Well, spiritualistic, mediumistic, and supernatural phenomena in general.

PROFESSOR. The question is, what do we consider supernatural? When, not a living man but a piece of stone attracted a nail to itself, how did the phenomena strike the first observers? As something natural? Or supernatural?

SAHATOF. Well, of course; but phenomena such as the magnet attracting iron always repeat themselves.

PROFESSOR. It is just the same in this case. The phenomenon repeats itself and we experiment with it. And not only that, but we apply to the phenomena we are investigating the laws common to other phenomena. These phenomena seem supernatural only because their causes are attributed to the medium himself. But that is where the mistake lies. The phenomena are not caused by the medium, but by psychic energy acting through a medium, and that is a very different thing. The whole matter lies in the law of equivalents.

SAHATOF. Yes, certainly, but ...

[Enter Tanya, who hides behind the hangings.]

LEONID FYODORITCH. Only remember that we cannot reckon on any results with certainty, with this medium any more than with Home or Kaptchitch. We may not succeed, but on the other hand we may even have perfect materialisation.

SAHATOF. Materialisation even? What do you mean by materialisation?

LEONID FYODORITCH. Why, I mean that some one who is dead, say, your father or your grandfather, may appear, take you by the hand, or give you something; or else some one may suddenly rise into the air, as happened to Alexey Vladimiritch last time.

PROFESSOR. Of course, of course. But the chief thing is the explanation of the phenomena, and the application to them of general laws.

[Enter the Fat Lady.]

FAT LADY. Anna Pavlovna has allowed me to join you.

LEONID FYODORITCH. Very pleased.

FAT LADY. Oh, how tired Grossman seems! He could scarcely hold his cup. Did you notice [to the Professor] how pale he turned at the moment he approached the hiding-place? I noticed it at once, and was the first to mention it to Anna Pavlovna.

PROFESSOR. Undoubtedly, loss of vital energy.

FAT LADY. Yes, it's just as I say, one should not abuse that sort of thing. You know, a hypnotist once suggested to a friend of mine, Vera Konshin (oh, you know her, of course) well, he suggested that she should leave off smoking, and her back began to ache!

PROFESSOR [trying to have his say] The temperature and the pulse clearly indicate ...

FAT LADY. One moment! Allow me! Well, I said to her: it's better to smoke than to suffer so with one's nerves. Of course, smoking is injurious; I should like to give it up myself, but, do what I will, I can't! Once I managed not to smoke for a fortnight, but could hold out no longer.

PROFESSOR [again trying to speak] Clearly proves ...

FAT LADY. Yes, no! Allow me, just one word! You say, "loss of strength." And I was also going to say that, when I travelled with post-horses ... the roads used to be dreadful in those days, you don't remember but I have noticed that all our nervousness comes from railways! I, for instance, can't sleep while travelling; I cannot fall asleep to save my life!

PROFESSOR [makes another attempt, which the Fat Lady baffles] The loss of strength ...

SAHATOF [smiling] Yes; oh yes!

[Leonid Fyodoritch rings.]

FAT LADY. I am awake one night, and another, and a third, and still I can't sleep!

[Enter Gregory.]

LEONID FYODORITCH. Please tell Theodore to get everything ready for the seance, and send Simon here, Simon, the butler's assistant, do you hear?

GREGORY. Yes, sir. [Exit].

PROFESSOR [to Sahatof]. The observation of the temperature and the pulse have shown loss of vital energy. The same will happen in consequence of the mediumistic phenomena. The law of the conservation of energy ...

FAT LADY. Oh yes, yes; I was just going to say that I am very glad that a simple peasant turns out to be a medium. That's very good. I always did say that the Slavophils ...

LEONID FYODORITCH. Let's go into the drawing-room in the meantime.

FAT LADY. Allow me, just one word! The Slavophils are right; but I always told my husband that one ought never to exaggerate anything! "The golden mean," you know. What is the use of maintaining that the common people are all perfect, when I have myself seen ...

LEONID FYODORITCH. Won't you come into the drawing-room?

FAT LADY. A boy, that high, who drank! I gave him a scolding at once. And he was grateful to me afterwards. They are children, and, as I always say, children need both love and severity!

[Exeunt all, all talking together.]

[Tanya enters from behind the hangings.]

TANYA. Oh, if it would only succeed! [Begins fastening some threads].

[Enter Betsy hurriedly.]

BETSY. Isn't papa here? [Looks inquiringly at Tanya] What are you doing here?

TANYA. Oh, Miss Elizabeth, I have only just come; I only wished ... only came in ... [Embarrassed].

BETSY. But they are going to have a seance here directly. [Notices Tanya drawing in the threads, looks at her, and suddenly bursts out laughing] Tanya! Why, it's you who do it all? Now don't deny it. And last time it was you too? Yes, it was, it was!

TANYA. Miss Elizabeth, dearest!

BETSY [delighted] Oh, that is a joke! Well, I never. But why do you do it?

TANYA. Oh miss, dear miss, don't betray me!

BETSY. Not for the world! I'm awfully glad. Only tell me how you manage it?

TANYA. Well, I just hide, and then, when it's all dark, I come out and do it. That's how.

BETSY [pointing to threads] And what is this for? You needn't tell me. I see; you draw ...

TANYA. Miss Elizabeth, darling! I will confess it, but only to you. I used to do it just for fun, but now I mean business.

BETSY. What? How? What business?

TANYA. Well, you see, those peasants that came this morning, you saw them. They want to buy some land, and your father won't sell it; well, and Theodore Ivanitch, he says it's the spirits as forbid him. So I have had a thought as ...

BETSY. Oh, I see! Well, you are a clever girl! Do it, do it.... But how will you manage it?

TANYA. Well, I thought, when they put out the lights, I'll at once begin knocking and shying things about, touching their heads with the threads, and at last I'll take the paper about the land and throw it on the table. I've got it here.

BETSY. Well, and then?

TANYA. Why, don't you see? They will be astonished. The peasants had the paper, and now it's here. I will teach ...

BETSY. Why, of course! Simon is the medium to-day!

TANYA. Well, I'll teach him ... [Laughs so that she can't continue] I'll tell him to squeeze with his hands any one he can get hold of! Of course, not your father, he'd never dare do that, but any one else; he'll squeeze till it's signed.

BETSY [laughing] But that's not the way it is done. Mediums never do anything themselves.

TANYA. Oh, never mind. It's all one; I daresay it'll turn out all right.

[Enter Theodore Ivanitch.]

[Exit Betsy, making signs to Tanya.]

THEODORE IVANITCH. Why are you here?

TANYA. It's you I want, Theodore Ivanitch, dear ...

THEODORE IVANITCH. Well, what is it?

TANYA. About that affair of mine as I spoke of.

THEODORE IVANITCH [laughs] I've made the match; yes, I've made the match. The matter is settled; we have shaken hands on it, only not had a drink on it.

TANYA [with a shriek] Never! So it's all right?

THEODORE IVANITCH. Don't I tell you so? He says, "I shall consult the missus, and then, God willing"

TANYA. Is that what he said? [Shrieks] Dear Theodore Ivanitch, I'll pray for you all the days of my life!

THEODORE IVANITCH. All right! All right! Now is not the time. I've been ordered to arrange the room for the seance.

TANYA. Let me help you. How's it to be arranged?

THEODORE IVANITCH. How? Why, the table in the middle of the room, chairs, the guitar, the accordion. The lamp is not wanted, only candles.

TANYA [helps Theodore Ivanitch to place the things] Is that right? The guitar here, and here the inkstand. [Places it] So?

THEODORE IVANITCH. Can it be true that they'll make Simon sit here?

TANYA. I suppose so; they've done it once.

THEODORE IVANITCH. Wonderful! [Puts on his pince-nez] But is he clean?

TANYA. How should I know?

THEODORE IVANITCH. Then, I'll tell you what ...

TANYA. Yes, Theodore Ivanitch?

THEODORE IVANITCH. Go and take a nail-brush and some Pears' soap; you may take mine ... and go and cut his claws and scrub his hands as clean as possible.

TANYA. He can do it himself.

THEODORE IVANITCH. Well then, tell him to. And tell him to put on a clean shirt as well.

TANYA. All right, Theodore Ivanitch. [Exit].

THEODORE IVANITCH [sits down in an easy-chair] They're educated and learned, Alexey Vladimiritch now, he's a professor and yet sometimes one can't help doubting very much. The people's rude superstitions are being abolished: hobgoblins, sorcerers, witches.... But if one considers it, is not this equally superstitious? How is it possible that the souls of the dead should come and talk, and play the guitar? No! Some one is fooling them, or they are fooling themselves. And as to this business with Simon, it's simply incomprehensible. [Looks at an album] Here's their spiritualistic album. How is it possible to photograph a spirit? But here is the likeness of a Turk and Leonid Fyodoritch sitting by.... Extraordinary human weakness!

[Enter Leonid Fyodoritch.]

LEONID FYODORITCH. Is it all ready?

THEODORE IVANITCH [rising leisurely] Quite ready. [Smiles] Only I don't know about your new medium. I hope he won't disgrace you, Leonid Fyodoritch.

LEONID FYODORITCH. No, I and Alexey Vladimiritch have tested him. He is a wonderfully powerful medium!

THEODORE IVANITCH. Well, I don't know. But is he clean enough? I don't suppose you have thought of ordering him to wash his hands? It might be rather inconvenient.

LEONID FYODORITCH. His hands? Oh yes! They're not clean, you think?

THEODORE IVANITCH. What can you expect? He's a peasant, and there will be ladies present, and Marya Vasilevna.

LEONID FYODORITCH. It will be all right.

THEODORE IVANITCH. And then I have something to report to you. Timothy, the coachman, complains that he can't keep things clean because of the dogs.

LEONID FYODORITCH [arranging the things on the table absent-mindedly] What dogs?

THEODORE IVANITCH. The three hounds that came for Vasily Leoniditch to-day.

LEONID FYODORITCH [vexed] Tell Anna Pavlovna! She can do as she likes about it. I have no time.

THEODORE IVANITCH. But you know her weakness ...

LEONID FYODORITCH. 'Tis just as she likes, let her do as she pleases. As for him, one never gets anything but unpleasantness from him. Besides, I am busy.

[Enter Simon, smiling; he has a sleeveless peasant's coat on.]

SIMON. I was ordered to come.

LEONID FYODORITCH. Yes, it's all right. Let me see your hands. That will do, that will do very well! Well then, my good fellow, you must do just as you did before, sit down, and give way to your mood. But don't think at all.

SIMON. Why should I think? The more one thinks, the worse it is.

LEONID FYODORITCH. Just so, just so, exactly! The less conscious one is, the greater is the power. Don't think, but give in to your mood. If you wish to sleep, sleep; if you wish to walk, walk. Do you understand?

SIMON. How could one help understanding? It's simple enough.

LEONID FYODORITCH. But above all, don't be frightened. Because you might be surprised yourself. You must understand that just as we live here, so a whole world of invisible spirits live here also.

THEODORE IVANITCH [improving on what Leonid Fyodoritch has said] Invisible feelings, do you understand?

SIMON [laughs] How can one help understanding! It's very plain as you put it.

LEONID FYODORITCH. You may rise up in the air, or something of the kind, but don't be frightened.

SIMON. Why should I be frightened? That won't matter at all.

LEONID FYODORITCH. Well then, I'll go and call them all.... Is everything ready?

THEODORE IVANITCH. I think so.

LEONID FYODORITCH. But the slates?

THEODORE IVANITCH. They are downstairs. I'll bring them. [Exit].

LEONID FYODORITCH. All right then. So don't be afraid, but be at your ease.

SIMON. Had I not better take off my coat? One would be more easy like.

LEONID FYODORITCH. Your coat? Oh no. Don't take that off. [Exit].

SIMON. She tells me to do the same again, and she will again shy things about. How isn't she afraid?

[Enter Tanya in her stockings and in a dress of the colour of the wall-paper. Simon laughs.]

TANYA. Shsh!... They'll hear! There, stick these matches on your fingers as before. [Sticks them on] Well, do you remember everything?

SIMON [bending his fingers in, one by one] First of all, wet the matches and wave my hands about, that's one. Then make my teeth chatter, like this ... that's two. But I've forgotten the third thing.

TANYA. And it's the third as is the chief thing. Don't forget as soon as the paper falls on the table, I shall ring the little bell, then you do like this.... Spread your arms out far and catch hold of some one, whoever it is as sits nearest, and catch hold of him. And then squeeze! [Laughs] Whether it's a gentleman or a lady, it's all one; you just squeeze 'em, and don't let 'em go, as if it were in your sleep, and chatter with your teeth, or else howl like this. [Howls sotto-voce] And when I begin to play on the guitar, then stretch yourself as if you were waking up, you know.... Will you remember everything?

SIMON. Yes, I'll remember, but it is too funny.

TANYA. But mind you don't laugh. Still, it won't matter much if you do laugh; they'd think it was in your sleep. Only take care you don't really fall asleep when they put out the lights.

SIMON. No fear, I'll pinch my ears.

TANYA. Well then Sim darling, only mind do as I tell you, and don't get frightened. He'll sign the paper, see if he don't! They're coming!

[Gets under the sofa.]

[Enter Grossman and the Professor, Leonid Fyodoritch and the Fat Lady, the Doctor, Sahatof and Anna Pavlovna. Simon stands near the door.]

LEONID FYODORITCH. Please come in, all you doubters! Though we have a new and accidentally discovered medium, I expect very important phenomena to-night.

SAHATOF. That's very, very interesting.

FAT LADY [pointing to Simon] Mais il est tres bien![12]

[Note 12: FAT LADY. But he looks quite nice.]

ANNA PAVLOVNA. Yes, as a butler's assistant, but hardly ...

SAHATOF. Wives never have any faith in their husbands' work. You don't believe in anything of this kind?

ANNA PAVLOVNA. Of course not. Kaptchitch, it is true, has something exceptional about him, but Heaven knows what all this is about!

FAT LADY. No, Anna Pavlovna, permit me, you can't decide it in such a way. Before I was married, I once had a remarkable dream. Dreams, you know, are often such that you don't know where they begin and where they end; it was just such a dream that I ...

[Enter Vasily Leoniditch and Petristchef.]

FAT LADY. And much was revealed to me by that dream. Nowadays the young people [points to Petristchef and Vasily Leoniditch] deny everything.

VASILY LEONIDITCH. But look here, you know, now I, for instance, never deny anything! Eh, what?

[Betsy and Marya Konstantinovna enter, and begin talking to Petristchef.]

FAT LADY. And how can one deny the supernatural? They say it is unreasonable. But what if one's reason is stupid; what then? There now, on Garden Street, you know ... why, well, it appeared every evening! My husband's brother, what do you call him? Not beau-frere- what's the other name for it? I never can remember the names of these different relationships, well, he went there three nights running, and still he saw nothing; so I said to him ...

LEONID FYODORITCH. Well, who is going to stay here?

FAT LADY. I! I!

SAHATOF. I.

ANNA PAVLOVNA [to Doctor] Do you mean to say you are going to stay?

DOCTOR. Yes; I must see, if only once, what it is that Alexey Vladimiritch has discovered in it. How can we deny anything without proofs?

ANNA PAVLOVNA. Then I am to take it to-night for certain?

DOCTOR. Take what?... Oh, the powder. Yes, it would perhaps be better. Yes, yes, take it.... However, I shall come upstairs again.

ANNA PAVLOVNA. Yes please, do. [Loud] When it is over, mesdames et messieurs, I shall expect you to come to me upstairs to rest from your emotions, and then we will finish our rubber.

FAT LADY. Oh, certainly.

SAHATOF. Yes, thanks!

[Exit Anna Pavlovna.]

BETSY [to Petristchef] You must stay, I tell you. I promise you something extraordinary. Will you bet?

MARYA KONSTANTINOVNA. But you don't believe in it?

BETSY. To-day I do.

MARYA KONSTANTINOVNA [to Petristchef] And do you believe?

PETRISTCHEF. "I can't believe, I cannot trust a heart for falsehood framed." Still, if Elizabeth Leonidovna commands ...

VASILY LEONIDITCH. Let us stay, Marya Konstantinovna. Eh, what? I shall invent something epatant.

MARYA KONSTANTINOVNA. No, you mustn't make me laugh. You know I can't restrain myself.

VASILY LEONIDITCH [loud] I remain!

LEONID FYODORITCH [severely] But I beg those who remain not to joke about it. It is a serious matter.

PETRISTCHEF. Do you hear? Well then, let's stay. Vovo, sit here, and don't be too shy.

BETSY. Yes, it's all very well for you to laugh; but just wait till you see what will happen.

VASILY LEONIDITCH. Oh, but supposing it's true? Won't it be a go! Eh, what?

PETRISTCHEF [trembles] Oh, I'm afraid, I'm afraid! Marya Konstantinovna, I'm afraid! My tootsies tremble.

BETSY [laughing] Not so loud.

[All sit down.]

LEONID FYODORITCH. Take your seats, take your seats. Simon, sit down!

SIMON. Yes, sir. [Sits down on the edge of the chair].

LEONID FYODORITCH. Sit properly.

PROFESSOR. Sit straight in the middle of the chair, and quite at your ease. [Arranges Simon on his chair].

[Betsy, Marya Konstantinovna and Vasily Leoniditch laugh.]

LEONID FYODORITCH [raising his voice] I beg those who are going to remain here not to behave frivolously, but to regard this matter seriously, or bad results might follow. Do you hear, Vovo! If you can't be quiet, go away!

VASILY LEONIDITCH. Quite quiet! [Hides behind Fat Lady].

LEONID FYODORITCH. Alexey Vladimiritch, will you mesmerise him?

PROFESSOR. No; why should I do it when Anton Borisitch is here? He has had far more practice and has more power in that department than I.... Anton Borisitch!

GROSSMAN. Ladies and gentlemen, I am not, strictly speaking, a spiritualist. I have only studied hypnotism. It is true I have studied hypnotism in all its known manifestations; but what is called spiritualism, is entirely unknown to me. When a subject is thrown into a trance, I may expect the hypnotic phenomena known to me: lethargy, abulia, anæsthesia, analgesia, catalepsy, and every kind of susceptibility to suggestion. Here it is not these but other phenomena we expect to observe. Therefore it would be well to know of what kind are the phenomena we expect to witness, and what is their scientific significance.

SAHATOF. I thoroughly agree with Mr. Grossman. Such an explanation would be very interesting.

LEONID FYODORITCH. I think Alexey Vladimiritch will not refuse to give us a short explanation.

PROFESSOR. Why not? I can give an explanation if it is desired. [To the Doctor] Will you kindly note his temperature and pulse? My explanation must, of necessity, be cursory and brief.

LEONID FYODORITCH. Yes, please; briefly, quite briefly.

DOCTOR. All right. [Takes out thermometer] Now then, my lad ... [Places the thermometer].

SIMON. Yes, sir!

PROFESSOR [rising and addressing the Fat Lady, then reseating himself] Ladies and gentlemen! The phenomenon we are investigating to-night is regarded, on the one hand, as something new; and, on the other, as something transcending the limits of natural conditions. Neither view is correct. This phenomenon is not new but is as old as the world; and it is not supernatural but is subject to the eternal laws that govern all that exists. This phenomenon has been usually defined as "intercourse with the spirit world." That definition is inexact. Under such a definition the spirit world is contrasted with the material world. But this is erroneous; there is no such contrast! Both worlds are so closely connected that it is impossible to draw a line of demarcation, separating the one from the other. We say, matter is composed of molecules ...

PETRISTCHEF. Prosy matter! [Whispering and laughter].

PROFESSOR [pauses, then continues] Molecules are composed of atoms, but the atoms, having no extension, are in reality nothing but the points of application of forces. Strictly speaking, not of forces but of energy, that same energy which is as much a unity and just as indestructible as matter. But matter, though one, has many different aspects, and the same is true of energy. Till recently only four forms of energy, convertible into one another, have been known to us: energies known as the dynamic, the thermal, the electric, and the chemic. But these four aspects of energy are far from exhausting all the varieties of its manifestation. The forms in which energy may manifest itself are very diverse, and it is one of these new and as yet but little known phases of energy, that we are investigating to-night. I refer to mediumistic energy.

[Renewed whispering and laughter among the young people.]

PROFESSOR [stops and casts a severe look round] Mediumistic energy has been known to mankind for ages: prophecy, presentiments, visions and so on, are nothing but manifestations of mediumistic energy. The manifestations produced by it have, I say, been known to mankind for ages. But the energy itself has not been recognised as such till quite recently, not till that medium, the vibrations of which cause the manifestations of mediumistic energy, was recognised. In the same way that the phenomena of light were inexplicable until the existence of an imponderable substance, an ether, was recognised, so mediumistic phenomena seemed mysterious until the now fully established fact was recognised, that between the particles of ether there exists another still more rarified imponderable substance not subject to the law of the three dimensions ...

[Renewed laughter, whispers, and giggling.]

PROFESSOR [again looks round severely] And just as mathematical calculations have irrefutably proved the existence of imponderable ether which gives rise to the phenomena of light and electricity, so the successive investigations of the ingenious Hermann, of Schmidt, and of Joseph Schmatzhofen, have confirmed beyond a doubt the existence of a substance which fills the universe and may be called spiritual ether.

FAT LADY. Ah, now I understand. I am so grateful ...

LEONID FYODORITCH. Yes, but Alexey Vladimiritch, could you not ... condense it a little?

PROFESSOR [not heeding the remark] And so, as I have just had the honour of mentioning to you, a succession of strictly scientific experiments have made plain to us the laws of mediumistic phenomena. These experiments have proved that, when certain individuals are plunged into a hypnotic state (a state differing from ordinary sleep only by the fact that man's physiological activity is not lowered by the hypnotic influence but, on the contrary, is always heightened, as we have recently witnessed) when, I say, any individual is plunged into such a state, this always produces certain perturbations in the spiritual ether, perturbations quite similar to those produced by plunging a solid body into liquid matter. These perturbations are what we call mediumistic phenomena ...

[Laughter, and whispers.]

SAHATOF. That is quite comprehensible and correct; but if, as you are kind enough to inform us, the plunging of the medium into a trance produces perturbations of the spiritual ether, allow me to ask why (as is usually supposed to be the case in spiritualistic seances) these perturbations result in an activity on the part of the souls of dead people?

PROFESSOR. It is because the molecules of this spiritual ether are nothing but the souls of the living, the dead, and the unborn, and any vibration of the spiritual ether must inevitably cause a certain vibration of its atoms. These atoms are nothing but human souls, which enter into communication with one another by means of these movements.

FAT LADY [to Sahatof] What is it that puzzles you? It is so simple.... Thank you so, so much!

LEONID FYODORITCH. I think everything has now been explained, and that we may commence.

DOCTOR. The fellow is in a perfectly normal condition: temperature 37 decimal 2, pulse 74.

PROFESSOR [takes out his pocket-book and notes this down] What I have just had the honour of explaining will be confirmed by the fact, which we shall presently have an opportunity of observing, that after the medium has been thrown into a trance his temperature and pulse will inevitably rise, just as occurs in cases of hypnotism.

LEONID FYODORITCH. Yes, yes. But excuse me a moment. I should like to reply to Sergey Ivanitch's question: How do we know we are in communication with the souls of the dead? We know it because the spirit that appears, plainly tells us, as simply as I am speaking to you, who he is, and why he has come, and whether all is well with him! At our last seance a Spaniard, Don Castillos, came to us, and he told us everything. He told us who he was, and when he died, and that he was suffering for having taken part in the Inquisition. He even told us what was happening to him at the very time that he was speaking to us, namely, that at the very time he was talking to us he had to be born again on earth, and, therefore, could not continue his conversation with us.... But you'll see for yourselves ...

FAT LADY [interrupting] Oh, how interesting! Perhaps the Spaniard was born in one of our houses and is a baby now!

LEONID FYODORITCH. Quite possibly.

PROFESSOR. I think it is time we began.

LEONID FYODORITCH. I was only going to say ...

PROFESSOR. It is getting late.

LEONID FYODORITCH. Very well. Then we will commence. Anton Borisitch, be so good as to hypnotise the medium.

GROSSMAN. What method would you like me to use? There are several methods. There is Braid's system, there is the Egyptian symbol, and there is Charcot's system.

LEONID FYODORITCH [to the Professor] I think it is quite immaterial.

PROFESSOR. Quite.

GROSSMAN. Then I will make use of my own method, which I showed in Odessa.

LEONID FYODORITCH. If you please!

[Grossman waves his arms above Simon. Simon closes his eyes and stretches himself.]

GROSSMAN [looking closely at him] He is falling asleep! He is asleep! A remarkably rapid occurrence of hypnosis. The subject has evidently already reached a state of anæsthesia. He is remarkable, an unusually impressionable subject, and might be subjected to interesting experiments!... [Sits down, rises, sits down again] Now one might run a needle into his arm. If you like ...

PROFESSOR [to Leonid Fyodoritch] Do you notice how the medium's trance acts on Grossman? He is beginning to vibrate.

LEONID FYODORITCH. Yes, yes ... can the lights be extinguished now?

SAHATOF. But why is darkness necessary?

PROFESSOR. Darkness? Because it is a condition of the manifestation of mediumistic energy, just as a given temperature is a condition necessary for certain manifestations of chemical or dynamic energy.

LEONID FYODORITCH. But not always. Manifestations have been observed by me, and by many others, both by candlelight and daylight.

PROFESSOR [interrupting] May the lights be put out?

LEONID FYODORITCH. Yes, certainly. [Puts out candles] Ladies and gentlemen! attention, if you please.

[Tanya gets from under the sofa and takes hold of a thread tied to a chandelier.]

PETRISTCHEF. I like that Spaniard! Just in the midst of a conversation, off he goes head downwards ... as the French say: piquer une tete.[13]

[Note 13: To take a header.]

BETSY. You just wait a bit, and see what will happen!

PETRISTCHEF. I have only one fear, and that is that Vovo may be moved by the spirit to grunt like a pig!

VASILY LEONIDITCH. Would you like me to? I will ...

LEONID FYODORITCH. Gentlemen! Silence, if you please!

[Silence. Simon licks the matches on his fingers and rubs his knuckles with them.]

LEONID FYODORITCH. A light! Do you see the light?

SAHATOF. A light? Yes, yes, I see; but allow me ...

FAT LADY. Where? Where? Oh dear, I did not see it! Ah, there it is. Oh!...

PROFESSOR [whispers to Leonid Fyodoritch, and points to Grossman, who is moving] Do you notice how he vibrates? It is the dual influence. [The light appears again].

LEONID FYODORITCH [to the Professor] It must be he, you know!

SAHATOF. Who?

LEONID FYODORITCH. A Greek, Nicholas. It is his light. Don't you think so, Alexey Vladimiritch?

SAHATOF. Who is this Greek, Nicholas?

PROFESSOR. A certain Greek, who was a monk at Constantinople under Constantine and who has been visiting us lately.

FAT LADY. Where is he? Where is he? I don't see him.

LEONID FYODORITCH. He is not yet visible ... Alexey Vladimiritch, he is particularly well disposed towards you. You question him.

PROFESSOR [in a peculiar voice] Nicholas! Is that you?

[Tanya raps twice on the wall.]

LEONID FYODORITCH [joyfully] It is he! It is he!

FAT LADY. Oh dear! Oh! I shall go away!

SAHATOF. Why do you suppose it is he?

LEONID FYODORITCH. Why, the two knocks. It is an affirmative answer; else all would have been silence.

[Silence. Suppressed giggling in the young people's corner. Tanya throws a lampshade, pencil and penwiper upon the table.]

LEONID FYODORITCH [whispers] Do you notice, gentlemen, here is a lamp-shade, and something else, a pencil!... Alexey Vladimiritch, it is a pencil!

PROFESSOR. All right, all right! I am watching both him and Grossman!

[Grossman rises and feels the things that have fallen on the table.]

SAHATOF. Excuse me, excuse me! I should like to see whether it is not the medium who is doing it all himself?

LEONID FYODORITCH. Do you think so? Well, sit by him and hold his hands. But you may be sure he is asleep.

SAHATOF [approaches. Tanya lets a thread touch his head. He is frightened, and stoops]. Ye ... ye ... yes! Strange, very strange! [Takes hold of Simon's elbow. Simon howls].

PROFESSOR [to Leonid Fyodoritch] Do you notice the effect of Grossman's presence? It is a new phenomenon, I must note it ... [Runs out to note it down, and returns again].

LEONID FYODORITCH. Yes.... But we cannot leave Nicholas without an answer. We must begin ...

GROSSMAN [rises, approaches Simon and raises and lowers his arm] It would be interesting to produce contraction! The subject is in profound hypnosis.

PROFESSOR [to Leonid Fyodoritch] Do you see? Do you see?

GROSSMAN. If you like ...

DOCTOR. Now then, my dear sir, leave the management to Alexey Vladimiritch, the affair is turning out serious.

PROFESSOR. Leave him alone, he [referring to Grossman] is talking in his sleep!

FAT LADY. How glad I now am that I resolved to be present! It is frightening, but all the same I am glad, for I always said to my husband ...

LEONID FYODORITCH. Silence, if you please.

[Tanya draws a thread over the Fat Lady's head.]

FAT LADY. Aie!

LEONID FYODORITCH. What? What is it?

FAT LADY. He took hold of my hair!

LEONID FYODORITCH [whispers] Never mind, don't be afraid, give him your hand. His hand will be cold, but I like it.

FAT LADY [hides her hands] Not for the world!

SAHATOF. Yes, it is strange, very strange!

LEONID FYODORITCH. He is here and is seeking for intercourse. Who wishes to put a question to him?

SAHATOF. I should like to put a question, if I may.

PROFESSOR. Please do.

SAHATOF. Do I believe or not?

[Tanya knocks twice.]

PROFESSOR. The answer is affirmative.

SAHATOF. Allow me to ask again. Have I a ten rouble note in my pocket?

[Tanya knocks several times and passes a thread over Sahatof's head.]

SAHATOF. Ah! [Seizes the thread and breaks it].

PROFESSOR. I should ask those present not to ask indefinite or trivial questions. It is unpleasant to him!

SAHATOF. No, but allow me! Here I have a thread in my hand!

LEONID FYODORITCH. A thread? Hold it fast; that happens often, and not only threads but sometimes even silk cords, very ancient ones!

SAHATOF. No, but where did this thread come from?

[Tanya throws a cushion at him.]

SAHATOF. Wait a bit; wait! Something soft has hit me on the head. Light a candle, there is something ...

PROFESSOR. We beg of you not to interrupt the manifestations.

FAT LADY. For goodness' sake don't interrupt! I should also like to ask something. May I?

LEONID FYODORITCH. Yes, if you like.

FAT LADY. I should like to ask about my digestion. May I? I want to know what to take: aconite or belladonna?

[Silence, whispers among the young people; suddenly Vasily Leoniditch begins to cry like a baby: "ou-a, ou-a!" [Laughter.] Holding their mouths and noses, the girls and Petristchef run away bursting with laughter.]

FAT LADY. Ah, that must be the monk who's been born again!

LEONID FYODORITCH [beside himself with anger, whispers] One gets nothing but tomfoolery from you! If you don't know how to behave decently, go away!

[Exit Vasily Leoniditch. Darkness and silence.]

FAT LADY. Oh, what a pity! Now one can't ask any more! He is born!

LEONID FYODORITCH. Not at all. It is only Vovo's nonsense. But he is here. Ask him.

PROFESSOR. That often happens. These jokes and ridicule are quite usual occurrences. I expect he is still here. But we may ask. Leonid Fyodoritch, will you?

LEONID FYODORITCH. No, you, if you please. This has upset me. So unpleasant! Such want of tact!...

PROFESSOR. Very well.... Nicholas, are you here?

[Tanya raps twice and rings. Simon roars, spreads his arms out, seizes Sahatof and the Professor, squeezing them.]

PROFESSOR. What an unexpected phenomenon! The medium himself reacted upon! This never happened before! Leonid Fyodoritch, will you watch? It is difficult for me to do so. He squeezes me so! Mind you observe Grossman! This needs the very greatest attention!

[Tanya throws the peasants' paper on the table.]

LEONID FYODORITCH. Something has fallen upon the table.

PROFESSOR. See what it is!

LEONID FYODORITCH. Paper! A folded paper!

[Tanya throws a travelling inkstand on the table.]

LEONID FYODORITCH. An inkstand!

[Tanya throws a pen.]

LEONID FYODORITCH. A pen!

[Simon roars and squeezes.]

PROFESSOR [crushed] Wait a bit, wait: a totally new manifestation! The action proceeding not from the mediumistic energy produced, but from the medium himself! However, open the inkstand, and put the pen on the table, and he will write!

[Tanya goes behind Leonid Fyodoritch and strikes him on the head with the guitar.]

LEONID FYODORITCH. He has struck me on the head! [Examining table] The pen is not writing yet and the paper remains folded.

PROFESSOR. See what the paper is, and quickly; evidently the dual influence, his and Grossman's, has produced a perturbation!

LEONID FYODORITCH [goes out and returns at once] Extraordinary! This paper is an agreement with some peasants that I refused to sign this morning and returned to the peasants. Probably he wants me to sign it?

PROFESSOR. Of course! Of course! But ask him.

LEONID FYODORITCH. Nicholas, do you wish ...

[Tanya knocks twice.]

PROFESSOR. Do you hear? It is quite evident!

[Leonid Fyodoritch takes the paper and pen and goes out. Tanya knocks, plays on the guitar and the accordion, and then creeps under the sofa. Leonid Fyodoritch returns. Simon stretches himself and coughs.]

LEONID FYODORITCH. He is waking up. We can light the candles.

PROFESSOR [hurriedly] Doctor, Doctor, please, his pulse and temperature! You will see that a rise of both will be apparent.

LEONID FYODORITCH [lights the candles] Well, what do you gentlemen who were sceptical think of it now?

DOCTOR [goes up to Simon and places thermometer] Now then my lad. Well, have you had a nap? There, put that in there, and give me your hand. [Looks at his watch].

SAHATOF [shrugging his shoulders] I must admit that all that has occurred cannot have been done by the medium. But the thread?... I should like the thread explained.

LEONID FYODORITCH. A thread! A thread! We have been witnessing manifestations more important than a thread.

SAHATOF. I don't know. At all events, je reserve mon opinion.

FAT LADY [to Sahatof] Oh no, how can you say: "je reserve mon opinion?" And the infant with the little wings? Didn't you see? At first I thought it was only an illusion, but afterwards it became clearer and clearer, like a live ...

SAHATOF. I can only speak of what I have seen. I did not see that, nothing of the kind.

FAT LADY. You don't mean to say so? Why, it was quite plainly visible! And to the left there was a monk clothed in black bending over it ...

SAHATOF [moves away. Aside] What exaggeration!

FAT LADY [addressing the Doctor] You must have seen it! It rose up from your side.

[Doctor goes on counting pulse without heeding her.]

FAT LADY [to Grossman] And that light, the light around it, especially around its little face! And the expression so mild and tender, something so heavenly! [Smiles tenderly herself].

GROSSMAN. I saw phosphorescent light, and objects changed their places, but I saw nothing more than that.

FAT LADY. Don't tell me! You don't mean it! It is simply that you scientists of Charcot's school do not believe in a life beyond the grave! As for me, no one could now make me disbelieve in a future life, no one in the world!

[Grossman moves away from her.]

FAT LADY. No, no, whatever you may say, this is one of the happiest moments of my life! When I heard Sarasate play, and now.... Yes! [No one listens to her. She goes up to Simon] Now tell me, my friend, what did you feel? Was it very trying?

SIMON [laughs] Yes, ma'm, just so.

FAT LADY. Still not unendurable?

SIMON. Just so, ma'm. [To Leonid Fyodoritch] Am I to go?

LEONID FYODORITCH. Yes, you may go.

DOCTOR [to the Professor] The pulse is the same, but the temperature is lower.

PROFESSOR. Lower! [Considers awhile, then suddenly divines the conclusion] It had to be so, it had to descend! The dual influence crossing had to produce some kind of reflex action. Yes, that's it!

[Exeunt, all talking at once.]

{ LEONID FYODORITCH. I'm only sorry we had no complete materialisation. But still.... Come, gentlemen, let us go to the drawing-room?
{
{ FAT LADY. What specially struck me was when he flapped his wings, and one saw how he rose!
{
{ GROSSMAN [to Sahatof] If we had kept to hypnotism, we might have produced a thorough state of epilepsy. The success might have been complete!
{
{ SAHATOF. It is very interesting, but not entirely convincing. That is all I can say.

[Enter Theodore Ivanitch.]

LEONID FYODORITCH [with paper in his hand] Ah, Theodore, what a remarkable seance we have had! It turns out that the peasants must have the land on their own terms.

THEODORE IVANITCH. Dear me!

LEONID FYODORITCH. Yes, indeed. [Showing paper] Fancy, this paper that I returned to them, suddenly appeared on the table! I have signed it.

THEODORE IVANITCH. How did it get there?

LEONID FYODORITCH. Well, it did get there! [Exit, Theodore Ivanitch follows him out].

TANYA [gets from under the sofa and laughs] Oh dear, oh dear! Well, I did get a fright when he got hold of the thread! [Shrieks] Well, anyhow, it's all right, he has signed it!

[Enter Gregory.]

GREGORY. So it was you that was fooling them?

TANYA. What business is it of yours?

GREGORY. And do you think the missis will be pleased with you for it? No, you bet; you're caught now! I'll tell them what tricks you're up to, if you don't let me have my way!

TANYA. And you'll not get your way, and you'll not do me any harm!

[Curtain.]

ACT IV

The same scene as in Act I. The next day. Two liveried footmen, Theodore Ivanitch and Gregory.

FIRST FOOTMAN [with grey whiskers] Yours is the third house to-day. Thank goodness that all the at-homes are in this direction. Yours used to be on Thursdays.

THEODORE IVANITCH. Yes, we changed to Saturday so as to be on the same day as the Golovkins and Grade von Grabes ...

SECOND FOOTMAN. The Stcherbakofs do the thing well. There's refreshments for the footmen every time they've a ball.

[The two Princesses, mother and daughter, come down the stairs accompanied by Betsy. The old Princess looks in her note-book and at her watch, and sits down on the settle. Gregory puts on her overshoes.]

YOUNG PRINCESS. Now, do come. Because, if you refuse, and Dodo refuses, the whole thing will be spoilt.

BETSY. I don't know. I must certainly go to the Shoúbins. And then there is the rehearsal.

YOUNG PRINCESS. You'll have plenty of time. Do, please. Ne nous fais pas faux bond.[14] Fedya and Koko will come.

[Note 14: Do not disappoint us.]

BETSY. J'en ai par-dessus la tete de votre Koko.[15]

[Note 15: BETSY. I have more than enough of your Koko.]

YOUNG PRINCESS. I thought I should see him here. Ordinairement il est d'une exactitude ...[16]

[Note 16: YOUNG PRINCESS. ... He is usually so very punctual ...]

BETSY. He is sure to come.

YOUNG PRINCESS. When I see you together, it always seems to me that he has either just proposed or is just going to propose.

BETSY. Yes, I don't suppose it can be avoided. I shall have to go through with it. And it is so unpleasant!

YOUNG PRINCESS. Poor Koko! He is head over ears in love.

BETSY. Cessez, les gens![17]

[Note 17: BETSY. Cease; mind the servants!]

[Young Princess sits down, talking in whispers. Gregory puts on her overshoes.]

YOUNG PRINCESS. Well then, good-bye till this evening.

BETSY. I'll try to come.

OLD PRINCESS. Then tell your papa that I don't believe in anything of the kind, but will come to see his new medium. Only he must let me know when. Good afternoon, ma toute belle. [Kisses Betsy, and exit, followed by her daughter. Betsy goes upstairs].

GREGORY. I don't like putting on an old woman's overshoes for her; she can't stoop, can't see her shoe for her stomach, and keeps poking her foot in the wrong place. It's different with a young one; it's pleasant to take her foot in one's hand.

SECOND FOOTMAN. Hear him! Making distinctions!

FIRST FOOTMAN. It's not for us footmen to make such distinctions.

GREGORY. Why shouldn't one make distinctions; are we not men? It's they think we don't understand! Just now they were deep in their talk, then they look at me, and at once it's "lay zhon!"

SECOND FOOTMAN. And what's that?

GREGORY. Oh, that means, "Don't talk, they understand!" It's the same at table. But I understand! You say, there's a difference? I say there is none.

FIRST FOOTMAN. There is a great difference for those who understand.

GREGORY. There is none at all. To-day I am a footman, and to-morrow I may be living no worse than they are. Has it never happened that they've married footmen? I'll go and have a smoke. [Exit].

SECOND FOOTMAN. That's a bold young man you've got.

THEODORE IVANITCH. A worthless fellow, not fit for service. He used to be an office boy and has got spoilt. I advised them not to take him, but the mistress liked him. He looks well on the carriage when they drive out.

FIRST FOOTMAN. I should like to send him to our Count; he'd put him in his place! Oh, he don't like those scatterbrains. "If you're a footman, be a footman and fulfil your calling." Such pride is not befitting.

[Petristchef comes running downstairs, and takes out a cigarette.]

PETRISTCHEF [deep in thought] Let's see, my second is the same as my first. Echo, a-co, co-coa. [Enter Koko Klingen, wearing his pince-nez] Ko-ko, co-coa. Cocoa tin, where do you spring from?

KOKO KLINGEN. From the Stcherbakofs. You are always playing the fool ...

PETRISTCHEF. No, listen to my charade. My first is the same as my second, my third may be cracked, my whole is like your pate.

KOKO KLINGEN. I give it up. I've no time.

PETRISTCHEF. Where else are you going?

KOKO KLINGEN. Where? Of course to the Ivins, to practise for the concert. Then to the Shoúbins, and then to the rehearsal. You'll be there too, won't you?

PETRISTCHEF. Most certainly. At the re-her-Sall and also at the re-her-Sarah. Why, at first I was a savage, and now I am both a savage and a general.

KOKO KLINGEN. How did yesterday's seance go off?

PETRISTCHEF. Screamingly funny! There was a peasant, and above all, it was all in the dark. Vovo cried like an infant, the Professor defined, and Marya Vasilevna refined. Such a lark! You ought to have been there.

KOKO KLINGEN. I'm afraid, mon cher. You have a way of getting off with a jest, but I always feel that if I say a word, they'll construe it into a proposal. Et ça ne m'arrange pas du tout, du tout. Mais du tout, du tout![18]

[Note 18: And that won't suit me at all, at all! Not at all, at all!]

PETRISTCHEF. Instead of a proposal, make a proposition, and receive a sentence! Well, I shall go in to Vovo's. If you'll call for me, we can go to the re-her-Sarah together.

KOKO KLINGEN. I can't think how you can be friends with such a fool. He is so stupid, a regular blockhead!

PETRISTCHEF. And I am fond of him. I love Vovo, but ... "with a love so strange, ne'er towards him the path untrod shall be" ... [Exit into Vovo's room].

[Betsy comes down with a Lady. Koko bows significantly to Betsy.]

BETSY [shaking Koko's hand without turning towards him. To Lady] You are acquainted?

LADY. No.

BETSY. Baron Klingen.... Why were you not here last night?

KOKO KLINGEN. I could not come, I was engaged.

BETSY. What a pity, it was so interesting! [Laughs] You should have seen what manifestations we had! Well, how is our charade getting on?

KOKO KLINGEN. Oh, the verses for mon second are ready. Nick composed the verses, and I the music.

BETSY. What are they? What are they? Do tell me!

KOKO KLINGEN. Wait a minute; how does it go?... Oh, the knight sings:
"Oh, naught so beautiful as nature:
The Nautilus sails by.
Oh, naughty lass, oh, naughty lass!
Oh, nought, oh nought! Oh fie!"

LADY. I see, my second is "nought," and what is my first?

KOKO KLINGEN. My first is Aero, the name of a girl savage.

BETSY. Aero, you see, is a savage who wished to devour the object of her love. [Laughs] She goes about lamenting, and sings
"My appetite,"

KOKO KLINGEN [interrupts]
"How can I fight," ...

BETSY [chimes in]
"Some one to chew I long.
I seeking go ..."

KOKO KLINGEN
"But even so ..."

BETSY
"No one to chew can find."

KOKO KLINGEN
"A raft sails by,"

BETSY
"It cometh nigh;
Two generals upon it ..."

KOKO KLINGEN
"Two generals are we:
By fate's hard decree,
To this island we flee."

And then, the refrain

"By fate's hard decree,
To this island we flee."

LADY. Charmant!

BETSY. But just think how silly!

KOKO KLINGEN. Yes, that's the charm of it!

LADY. And who is to be Aero?

BETSY. I am. And I have had a costume made, but mamma says it's "not decent." And it is not a bit less decent than a ball dress. [To Theodore Ivanitch] Is Bourdier's man here?

THEODORE IVANITCH. Yes, he is waiting in the kitchen.

LADY. Well, and how will you represent Aeronaut?

BETSY. Oh, you'll see. I don't want to spoil the pleasure for you. Au revoir.

LADY. Good-bye! [They bow. Exit Lady].

BETSY [to Koko Klingen] Come up to mamma.

Betsy and Koko go upstairs. Jacob enters from servants' quarters, carrying a tray with teacups, cakes, &c., and goes panting across the stage.

JACOB [to the Footmen] How d'you do? How d'you do? [Footmen bow].

JACOB [to Theodore Ivanitch] Couldn't you tell Gregory to help a bit! I'm ready to drop.... [Exit up the stairs].

FIRST FOOTMAN. That is a hard-working chap you've got there.

THEODORE IVANITCH. Yes, a good fellow. But there now, he doesn't satisfy the mistress, she says his appearance is ungainly. And now they've gone and told tales about him for letting some peasants into the kitchen yesterday. It is a bad look-out: they may dismiss him. And he is a good fellow.

SECOND FOOTMAN. What peasants were they?

THEODORE IVANITCH. Peasants that had come from our Koursk village to buy some land. It was night, and they were our fellow-countrymen, one of them the father of the butler's assistant. Well, so they were asked into the kitchen. It so happened that there was thought-reading going on. Something was hidden in the kitchen, and all the gentlefolk came down, and the mistress saw the peasants. There was such a row! "How is this," she says; "these people may be infected, and they are let into the kitchen!" ... She is terribly afraid of this infection.

[Enter Gregory.]

THEODORE IVANITCH. Gregory, you go and help Jacob. I'll stay here. He can't manage alone.

GREGORY. He's awkward, that's why he can't manage. [Exit].

FIRST FOOTMAN. And what is this new mania they have got? This infection!... So yours also is afraid of it?

THEODORE IVANITCH. She fears it worse than fire! Our chief business, nowadays, is fumigating, washing, and sprinkling.

FIRST FOOTMAN. I see. That's why there is such a stuffy smell here. [With animation] I don't know what we're coming to with these infection notions. It's just destable! They seem to have forgotten the Lord. There's our master's sister, Princess Mosolova, her daughter was dying and, will you believe it, neither father nor mother would come near her! So she died without their having taken leave of her. And the daughter cried, and called them to say good-bye, but they didn't go! The doctor had discovered some infection or other! And yet their own maid and a trained nurse were with her, and nothing happened to them; they're still alive!

[Enter Vasily Leoniditch and Petristchef from Vasily Leoniditch's room, smoking cigarettes.]

PETRISTCHEF. Come along then, only I must take Koko, Cocoanut, with me.

VASILY LEONIDITCH. Your Koko is a regular dolt; I can't bear him. A hare-brained fellow, a regular gad-about! Without any kind of occupation, eternally loafing around! Eh, what?

PETRISTCHEF. Well, anyhow, wait a bit, I must say good-bye.

VASILY LEONIDITCH. All right. And I will go and look at my dogs in the coachman's room. I've got a dog there that's so savage, the coachman said, he nearly ate him.

PETRISTCHEF. Who ate whom? Did the coachman really eat the dog?

VASILY LEONIDITCH. You are always at it! [Puts on outdoor things and goes out].

PETRISTCHEF [thoughtfully] Ma-kin-tosh, Co-co-tin.... Let's see. [Goes upstairs].

[Jacob runs across the stage.]

THEODORE IVANITCH. What's the matter?

JACOB. There is no more thin bread and butter. I said ... [Exit].

SECOND FOOTMAN. And then our master's little son fell ill, and they sent him at once to an hotel with his nurse, and there he died without his mother.

FIRST FOOTMAN. They don't seem to fear sin! I think you cannot escape from God anywhere.

THEODORE IVANITCH. That's what I think.

[Jacob runs upstairs with bread and butter.]

FIRST FOOTMAN. One should consider too, that if we are to be afraid of everybody like that, we'd better shut ourselves up within four walls, as in a prison, and stick there!

[Enter Tanya; she bows to the Footmen.]

TANYA. Good afternoon.

[Footmen bow.]

TANYA. Theodore Ivanitch, I have a word to say to you.

THEODORE IVANITCH. Well, what?

TANYA. The peasants have come again, Theodore Ivanitch ...

THEODORE IVANITCH. Well? I gave the paper to Simon.

TANYA. I have given them the paper. They were that grateful! I can't say how! Now they only ask you to take the money.

THEODORE IVANITCH. But where are they?

TANYA. Here, by the porch.

THEODORE IVANITCH. All right, I'll tell the master.

TANYA. I have another request to you, dear Theodore Ivanitch.

THEODORE IVANITCH. What now?

TANYA. Why, don't you see, Theodore Ivanitch, I can't remain here any longer. Ask them to let me go.

[Enter Jacob, running.]

THEODORE IVANITCH [to Jacob] What d'you want?

JACOB. Another samovar, and oranges.

THEODORE IVANITCH. Ask the housekeeper.

[Exit Jacob.]

THEODORE IVANITCH [to Tanya] How is that?

TANYA. Why, don't you see, my position is such ...

JACOB [runs in] There are not enough oranges.

THEODORE IVANITCH. Serve up as many as you've got [Exit Jacob]. Now's not the time! Just see what a bustle we are in.

TANYA. But you know yourself, Theodore Ivanitch, there is no end to this bustle; one might wait for ever, you know yourself, and my affair is for life.... Dear Theodore Ivanitch, you have done me a good turn, be a father to me now, choose the right moment and tell her, or else she'll get angry and won't let me have my passport.[19]

[Note 19: Employers have charge of the servants' passports, and in this way have a hold on them in case of misconduct.]

THEODORE IVANITCH. Where's the hurry?

TANYA. Why, Theodore Ivanitch, it's all settled now.... And I could go to my godmother's and get ready, and then after Easter we'd get married.[20] Do tell her, dear Theodore Ivanitch!

[Note 20: See footnote, It is customary for peasants to marry just after Easter, but when spring has come and the field work begun, no marriages take place among them till autumn.]

THEODORE IVANITCH. Go away, this is not the place.

[An elderly Gentleman comes downstairs, puts on overcoat, and goes out followed by the Second Footman.]

[Exit Tanya. Enter Jacob.]

JACOB. Just fancy, Theodore Ivanitch, it's too bad! She wants to discharge me now! She says, "You break everything, and forget Frisk, and you let the peasants into the kitchen against my orders!" And you know very well that I knew nothing about it. Tatyana told me, "Take them into the kitchen"; how could I tell whose order it was?

THEODORE IVANITCH. Did the mistress speak to you?

JACOB. She's just spoken. Do speak up for me, Theodore Ivanitch! You see, my people in the country are only just getting on their feet, and suppose I lose my place, when shall I get another? Theodore Ivanitch, do, please!

[Anna Pavlovna comes down with the old Countess, whom she is seeing off. The Countess has false teeth and hair. The First Footman helps the Countess into her outdoor things.]

ANNA PAVLOVNA. Oh, most certainly, of course! I am so deeply touched.

COUNTESS. If it were not for my illness, I should come oftener to see you.

ANNA PAVLOVNA. You should really consult Peter Petrovitch. He is rough, but nobody can soothe one as he does. He is so clear, so simple.

COUNTESS. Oh no, I shall keep to the one I am used to.

ANNA PAVLOVNA. Pray, take care of yourself.

COUNTESS. Merci, mille fois merci.[21]

[Note 21: COUNTESS. Thank you (for your hospitality), a thousand thanks.]

[Gregory, dishevelled and excited, jumps out from the servants' quarters. Simon appears behind him in the doorway.]

SIMON. You'd better leave her alone!

GREGORY. You rascal! I'll teach you how to fight, you scamp, you!

ANNA PAVLOVNA. What do you mean? Do you think you are in a public-house?

GREGORY. This coarse peasant makes life impossible for me.

ANNA PAVLOVNA [provoked] You've lost your senses. Don't you see? [To Countess] Merci, mille fois merci. A mardi![22]

[Note 22: ANNA PAVLOVNA. Thank you (for coming to see us), a thousand thanks. Till next Tuesday!]

[Exeunt Countess and First Footman.]

ANNA PAVLOVNA [to Gregory] What is the meaning of this?

GREGORY. Though I do occupy the position of a footman, still I won't allow every peasant to hit me; I have my pride too.

ANNA PAVLOVNA. Why, what has happened?

GREGORY. Why, this Simon of yours has got so brave, sitting with the gentlemen, that he wants to fight!

ANNA PAVLOVNA. Why? What for?

GREGORY. Heaven only knows!

ANNA PAVLOVNA [to Simon] What is the meaning of it?

SIMON. Why does he bother her?

ANNA PAVLOVNA. What has happened?

SIMON [smiles] Well, you see, he is always catching hold of Tanya, the lady's-maid, and she won't have it. Well, so I just moved him aside a bit, just so, with my hand.

GREGORY. A nice little bit! He's almost caved my ribs in, and has torn my dress-coat, and he says, "The same power as came over me yesterday comes on me again," and he begins to squeeze me.

ANNA PAVLOVNA [to Simon] How dare you fight in my house?

THEODORE IVANITCH. May I explain it to you, ma'am? I must tell you Simon is not indifferent to Tanya, and is engaged to her. And Gregory, one must admit the truth, does not behave properly, nor honestly, to her. Well, so I suppose Simon got angry with him.

GREGORY. Not at all! It is all his spite, because I have discovered their trickery.

ANNA PAVLOVNA. What trickery?

GREGORY. Why, at the seance. All those things, last night, it was not Simon but Tanya who did them! I saw her getting out from under the sofa with my own eyes.

ANNA PAVLOVNA. What is that? From under the sofa?

GREGORY. I give you my word of honour. And it was she who threw the paper on the table. If it had not been for her the paper would not have been signed, nor the land sold to the peasants.

ANNA PAVLOVNA. And you saw it yourself?

GREGORY. With my own eyes. Shall I call her? She'll not deny it.

ANNA PAVLOVNA. Yes, call her.

[Exit Gregory.]

[Noise behind the scenes. The voice of the Doorkeeper, "No, no, you cannot." Doorkeeper is seen at the front door, the three Peasants rush in past him, the Second Peasant first; the Third one stumbles, falls on his nose, and catches hold of it.]

DOORKEEPER. You must not go in!

SECOND PEASANT. Where's the harm? We are not doing anything wrong. We only wish to pay the money!

FIRST PEASANT. That's just it; as by laying on the signature the affair is come to a conclusion, we only wish to make payment with thanks.

ANNA PAVLOVNA. Wait a bit with your thanks. It was all done by fraud! It is not settled yet. Not sold yet.... Leonid.... Call Leonid Fyodoritch. [Exit Doorkeeper].

Leonid Fyodoritch enters, but, seeing his wife and the Peasants, wishes to retreat.

ANNA PAVLOVNA. No, no, come here, please! I told you the land must not be sold on credit, and everybody told you so, but you let yourself be deceived like the veriest blockhead.

LEONID FYODORITCH. How? I don't understand who is deceiving?

ANNA PAVLOVNA. You ought to be ashamed of yourself! You have grey hair, and you let yourself be deceived and laughed at like a silly boy. You grudge your son some three hundred roubles which his social position demands, and let yourself be tricked of thousands, like a fool!

LEONID FYODORITCH. Now come, Annette, try to be calm.

FIRST PEASANT. We are only come about the acceptation of the sum, for example ...

THIRD PEASANT [taking out the money] Let us finish the matter, for Christ's sake!

ANNA PAVLOVNA. Wait, wait!

[Enter Tanya and Gregory.]

ANNA PAVLOVNA [angrily] You were in the small drawing-room during the seance last night?

[Tanya looks round at Theodore Ivanitch, Leonid Fyodoritch, and Simon, and sighs.]

GREGORY. It's no use beating about the bush; I saw you myself ...

ANNA PAVLOVNA. Tell me, were you there? I know all about it, so you'd better confess! I'll not do anything to you. I only want to expose him [pointing to Leonid Fyodoritch] your master.... Did you throw the paper on the table?

TANYA. I don't know how to answer. Only one thing, let me go home.

[Enter Betsy unobserved.]

ANNA PAVLOVNA [to Leonid Fyodoritch] There, you see! You are being made a fool of.

ANNA PAVLOVNA. There, you see! You are being made a fool of.]

TANYA. Let me go home, Anna Pavlovna!

ANNA PAVLOVNA. No, my dear! You may have caused us a loss of thousands of roubles. Land has been sold that ought not to be sold!

TANYA. Let me go, Anna Pavlovna!

ANNA PAVLOVNA. No; you'll have to answer for it! Such tricks won't do. We'll have you up before the Justice of the Peace!

BETSY [comes forward] Let her go, mamma. Or, if you wish to have her tried, you must have me tried too! She and I did it together.

ANNA PAVLOVNA. Well, of course, if you have a hand in anything, what can one expect but the very worst results!

[Enter the Professor.]

PROFESSOR. How do you do, Anna Pavlovna? How do you do, Miss Betsy? Leonid Fyodoritch, I have brought you a report of the Thirteenth Congress of Spiritualists at Chicago. An amazing speech by Schmidt!

LEONID FYODORITCH. Oh, that is interesting!

ANNA PAVLOVNA. I will tell you something much more interesting! It turns out that both you and my husband were fooled by this girl! Betsy takes it on herself, but that is only to annoy me. It was an illiterate peasant girl who fooled you, and you believed it all. There were no mediumistic phenomena last night; it was she [pointing to Tanya] who did it!

PROFESSOR [taking off his overcoat] What do you mean?

ANNA PAVLOVNA. I mean that it was she who, in the dark, played on the guitar and beat my husband on the head and performed all your idiotic tricks, and she has just confessed!

PROFESSOR [smiling] What does that prove?

ANNA PAVLOVNA. It proves that your mediumism is tomfoolery; that's what it proves!

PROFESSOR. Because this young girl wished to deceive, we are to conclude that mediumism is "tomfoolery," as you are pleased to express it? [Smiles] A curious conclusion! Very possibly this young girl may have wished to deceive: that often occurs. She may even have done something; but then, what she did she did. But the manifestations of mediumistic energy still remain manifestations of mediumistic energy! It is even very probable that what this young girl did, evoked (and so to say solicited) the manifestation of mediumistic energy, giving it a definite form.

ANNA PAVLOVNA. Another lecture!

PROFESSOR [sternly] You say, Anna Pavlovna, that this girl, and perhaps this dear young lady also, did something; but the light we all saw, and, in the first case the fall, and in the second the rise of temperature, and Grossman's excitement and vibration, were those things also done by this girl? And these are facts, Anna Pavlovna, facts! No! Anna Pavlovna, there are things which must be investigated and fully understood before they can be talked about, things too serious, too serious ...

LEONID FYODORITCH. And the child that Marya Vasilevna distinctly saw? Why, I saw it too.... That could not have been done by this girl.

ANNA PAVLOVNA. You think yourself wise, but you are a fool.

LEONID FYODORITCH. Well, I'm going.... Alexey Vladimiritch, will you come? [Exit into his study].

PROFESSOR [shrugging his shoulders, follows] Oh, how far, how far, we still lag behind Western Europe!

[Enter Jacob.]

ANNA PAVLOVNA [following Leonid Fyodoritch with her eyes] He has been tricked like a fool, and he sees nothing! [To Jacob] What do you want?

JACOB. How many persons am I to lay the table for?

ANNA PAVLOVNA. For how many?... Theodore Ivanitch! Let him give up the silver plate to you. Be off, at once! It is all his fault! This man will bring me to my grave. Last night he nearly starved the dog that had done him no harm! And, as if that were not enough, he lets the infected peasants into the kitchen, and now they are here again! It is all his fault! Be off at once! Discharge him, discharge him! [To Simon] And you, horrid peasant, if you dare to have rows in my house again, I'll teach you!

SECOND PEASANT. All right, if he is a horrid peasant there's no good keeping him; you'd better discharge him too, and there's an end of it.

ANNA PAVLOVNA [while listening to him looks at Third Peasant] Only look! Why, he has a rash on his nose, a rash! He is ill; he is a hotbed of infection!! Did I not give orders, yesterday, that they were not to be allowed into the house, and here they are again? Drive them out!

THEODORE IVANITCH. Then are we not to accept their money?

ANNA PAVLOVNA. Their money? Oh yes, take their money; but they must be turned out at once, especially this one! He is quite rotten!

THIRD PEASANT. That's not just, lady. God's my witness, it's not just! You'd better ask my old woman, let's say, whether I am rotten! I'm clear as crystal, let's say.

ANNA PAVLOVNA. He talks!... Off, off with him! It's all to spite me!... Oh, I can't bear it, I can't!... Send for the doctor! [Runs away, sobbing. Exit also Jacob and Gregory].

TANYA [to Betsy] Miss Elizabeth, darling, what am I to do now?

BETSY. Never mind, you go with them and I'll arrange it all. [Exit].

FIRST PEASANT. Well, your reverence, how about the reception of the sum now?

SECOND PEASANT. Let us settle up, and go.

THIRD PEASANT [fumbling with the packet of bank-notes] Had I known, I'd not have come for the world. It's worse than a fever!

THEODORE IVANITCH [to Doorkeeper] Show them into my room. There's a counting-board there. I'll receive their money. Now go.

DOORKEEPER. Come along.

THEODORE IVANITCH. And it's Tanya you have to thank for it. But for her you'd not have had the land.

FIRST PEASANT. That's just it. As she made the proposal, so she put it into effect.

THIRD PEASANT. She's made men of us. Else what were we? We had so little land, no room to let a hen out, let's say, not to mention the cattle. Good-bye, dear! When you get to the village, come to us and eat honey.

SECOND PEASANT. Let me get home and I'll start brewing the beer for the wedding! You will come?

TANYA. Yes, I'll come, I'll come! [Shrieks] Simon, this is fine, isn't it? [Exeunt Peasants].

THEODORE IVANITCH. Well, Tanya, when you have your house I'll come to visit you. Will you welcome me?

TANYA. Dear Theodore Ivanitch, just the same as we would our own father! [Embraces and kisses him].

[Curtain.]

Leo Tolstoy (1828-1910) – A Short Biography
Along with Feodor Dostoyevsky, Ivan Turgenev and Vladimir Nabokov, Leo Tolstoy is one of the most important pillars of Russian literature. He is mainly remembered for what is considered by many readers and critics as the greatest novel of all times, *War and Peace*. He is also the author of other successful novels such as *Anna Karenina* and *The Death of Ivan Ilyich*. His texts display his unique narratorial style and the strength of his descriptive techniques.

Tolstoy was born in 1828 in the Russian province of Tula to a noble family with considerable wealth. His Tula family estate, named Yasnaya Polyana, was transformed into The Tolstoy National Museum after his death. He was a brother to four other boys in the family. Their mother soon died to be followed by their father just a few years later and the children were confined to members of their father's family near the city of Kazan. As a young child, Tolstoy had home tutorials by private tutors who introduced him to the basics of reading and writing. He was not any brilliant, though. He rather showed early disinterest in formal education. When he was sent to the University of Kazan in 1843 to study oriental languages and then law, his lack of seriousness made him leave the university before receiving any degree. By that time, Tolstoy decided to go back home and manage his family's farm.

As a farmer, Tolstoy was very enthusiastic in his work. He treated his serfs as friends and even started teaching them before he built schools for them at a later stage. However, despite his great enthusiasm and vivacity, Tolstoy was not serious in farming either. He was a regular absentee. In fact, he was so fond of partying and socializing, a habit that suited his literary evasions more than it suited the labors of a true farmer. He started writing a diary during his farming years when one of his older brothers suggested that he joins him in the army. In the 1850s, Tolstoy had to take part in the Crimean War between Russia and an alliance of France, Britain and Ottoman Turkey. During his free time, he used to carry on with his diary. He eventually finished his first autobiographical book that he entitled *Childhood*. The publication of the latter in 1852 was an immediate success and was encouraged by publishers. It was then followed by a second part and a third part respectively entitled *Boyhood* (1854) and *Youth* (1857).

Apart from this autobiographical trilogy, Tolstoy also wrote about his experience in the army and the horrors and futility of wars. This was in *The Cossacks* that he finished later and published in 1862 and also in another trilogy entitled *Sevastopol Tales*. On Tolstoy's return home after the end of the Crimean war, he realized that he had already made himself a name that even the Tsar himself had heard about and appreciated. Yet, Tolstoy stubbornly refused to settle in Petersburg and join the Russian literary élite of the time. He rather chose to travel around Europe, visiting London and Paris and meeting with figures like Victor Hugo and Charles Darwin. He is even said to have attended some of the latter's historical lectures. Tolstoy's instability soon pushed him to return to Russia, though.

It was in the 1860s that Tolstoy started working on his masterpiece, *War and Peace*. An important part of it was first published in the famous periodical *The Russian Messenger* before it was finished in 1869. *War and Peace*, which was equally an immediate and everlasting success, was characterized by a large cast of characters representing real people that Tolstoy had actually met. Written in a rather epic style, the novel mainly described the horrors of war in concrete details from somebody who had a first-hand experience with killing and bloodshed. Though the story as well as the characters were fictional, the narrative developed in a very realistic way by recounting events from the Napoleonic Wars that took place in the very beginning of the 19th century. The novel was not only a seminal war fiction that would influence many a writer of the nineteenth and twentieth centuries, it also contained philosophical contemplation of universal issues related to the meaning and use of human conflicts.

After the phenomenal success of *War and Peace*, Tolstoy started working on his second most popular novel, *Anna Karenina*. A realistic novel too, the latter was first published in a series of installments in *The Russian Messenger* (1873-1877). The eponymous protagonist was a married woman belonging to aristocracy who had an affair with another man than her husband. The novel was hailed as a refined work of fiction by such important literary men as Nabokov, Dostoevsky and William Faulkner.

Such a huge success of his novels quickly made of Tolstoy a very rich man. His great wealth helped him realize many of his own dreams as well as the dreams of his young wife and his many children. However, money also became a source of trouble in his household. After the publication of *Anna Karenina*, Tolstoy was very concerned about his existential quest, trying to find a meaning and an objective for his life, something that he did not find in the Russian Orthodox Church. In a number of publications that followed, he explained his own personalized vision of the Christian faith. These works were "Confession" (1879), *The Mediator* (1883), *What I Believe* (1885) and "The Kingdom of God is Within You" (1894). Tolstoy's revolutionary views about faith and existence soon became popular and had followers not only in Russia, but also in other parts of the world. This influence made Russian authorities keep him under surveillance, mainly because he was critical of Russia's war policies as well as of the Orthodox Church and of the Tsar's religious role. Indeed, Tolstoy was among the advocates of the separation between Church and State.

One of the most remarkable characteristics of Tolstoy's reformed faith, if so to call it, was austerity and charity. He led a life of asceticism and vegetarianism and put his socialist ideals into practice by establishing numerous schools for the poor and funding public meals. He also believed that he had to give most of his fortunes away, which was strongly objected by his young wife. Generally, the latter did not appreciate her husband's new ideals and lifestyle, which caused serious misunderstandings between the couple towards Tolstoy's twilight years. By the end, the couple grudgingly came to an agreement according to which part of the wealth went to the wife.

Due to the effect of his war experiences, Tolstoy was also among the pioneers of the non-violent resistance of injustice. He strongly believed in pacifist actions and strategies of struggle. This made him become a source of inspiration for numerous political leaders, including his contemporary Mohandas Gandhi and later Martin Luther King, Jr.

Most of Tolstoy's later novels bore the influence of his rather new life of a mystic. He held convictions on the universality of faith, believing that "God is love." He realized the resemblances between different world religious traditions and mysticisms, including Christianity's various denominations, Buddhism, Judaism, Islam and Hinduism. For him, a common feature united all human faiths which was based on universal divine love. In 1886, Tolstoy published another bestselling title, *The Death of Ivan Ilyich*, which also represented a philosophical journey into questions about life, death and faith. *Father Sergius*, another novel that equally delves into questions of belief, was published in 1898. It was followed by *Resurrection* in 1989 and by *The Living Corpse* in 1890.

The year 1901 witnessed Tolstoy's excommunication from the Church and also his deselection from the Nobel Prize for Literature for uncertain reasons while he was incontestably the most qualified. Despite his extraordinary fame and worldwide success, Tolstoy's twilight years were marked by numerous problems. He had serious problems with his wife who disapproved of his religious transformation. He was tightly controlled by Russian authorities which feared his growing influence. He was also pursued by journalists and fans who did not allow him to enjoy a peaceful and intimate life. In addition to all this, Tolstoy started to suffer from old age and serious health problems.

In October 1910, Tolstoy decided to go on a pilgrimage, being accompanied by his daughter Aleksandra. Upon taking the train, the 82-year-old man did not stand the hardships of the trip and soon caught pneumonia. He resorted to the stationmaster's home in Astapovo which was not very far from Tolstoy's home itself. On November 9th, 1910, Leo Tolstoy passed away to be buried in his old estate Yasnaya Polyana.

www.ingramcontent.com/pod-product-compliance
Lightning Source LLC
Chambersburg PA
CBHW071328040426
42444CB00009B/2106